THE QUANTUM GODS

The cover illustration is from a painting by the author called 'Qabalah Mandala' and is a representation of the inner workings of the universe using the basic symbols of the Tarot, Astrology and Qabalah.

A mandala is traditionally used as an object of contemplation, its function being to aid the contemplator to integrate and synthesize the whole of his conceptual mind in one time and place and thus transcend it.

Jeff Love

THE QUANTUM GODS

The Origin and Nature of Matter and Consciousness

SAMUEL WEISER INC.   NEW YORK

First published in Great Britain 1976 by
The Compton Press Limited, Tisbury, Wiltshire

First American paperback edition 1979 by
Samuel Weiser, Inc.
740 Broadway
New York, N.Y. 10003

ISBN 0-87728-476-8

Printed in the U.S.A. by
Noble Offset Printers, Inc.
New York, N.Y. 10003

Contents

5 The World of Matter

6 The Co-Creation

7 The World of Ability

8 The World of Mind

9 The World of Body

10 The Body-Mind

PART THREE ENLIGHTENMENT INTENSIVE

11 Enlightenment, the Direct Experience of Truth

Preface

The Quantum Gods are beings of infinite ability. Yet each of them exists alone, unconscious of the existence of the others, and unable to manifest as a creative being.

It is only through the creation of a common reality that the Quantum Gods can attain consciousness of self and others. The Quantum Gods sign a contract of intent in which they invest their very existence in the formation of a co-created reality. They are motivated to sign the contract out of love – their desire to end their state of aloneness and to contact one another. The contract is written with the pen of intentionality on the paper of space-time in the ink of mass and energy. Their common reality is built of consciousness and a special condition of consciousness called matter. Matter is the medium; being is the message.

This is not a science fiction fantasy. The Quantum Gods are not ghosts, angels, or beings from another planet or time zone. This is a work of radical metaphysical philosophy unlike any other.

You and I are the Quantum Gods . . .

My grateful acknowledgement is due to A. G. M. Agmuller & Co., Switzerland, for permission to use their 'Swiss' Tarot cards in the cover illustration and to Builders of Adytum, Los Angeles, California, for their permission to quote from Paul Case's *The Book of Tokens.*

And my appreciation goes to John Moore and Edward Posey for their help and encouragement.

London, May 1976   J. L.

PART ONE
THE QABALISTIC
MODEL

1
The Path of the Dot

A story told in graphics, illustrating some of the basic premises of Qabalah

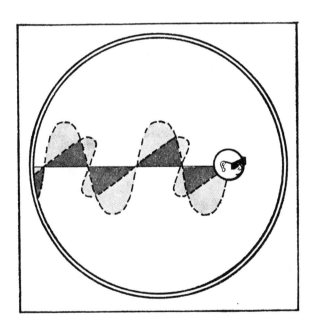

The dot represents the individual I AM
or Self

FROM NOTHING
COMES
EVERYTHING...

Consider the
opposite page as missing.
It represents the
primal state called

AYN

AYN means
ABSOLUTE
and
LIMITLESS
VOID
(no thingness)

The opposite page represents
the state called

AYN SOPH

AYN SOPH means
ENDLESS
and
BOUNDLESS
(infinity)

The opposite page represents
the state called

AYN SOPH AUR

which means
LIMITLESS LIGHT

The opposite page represents the three states of AYN, AYN SOPH, and AYN SOPH AUR superimposed on one another. The three states together are called

NEGATIVE EXISTENCE

Negative existence is the state which exists prior to all creation. It is the source of all finite and manifest things yet it remains

INFINITE AND UNMANIFEST

This is an enlargement of
NEGATIVE EXISTENCE

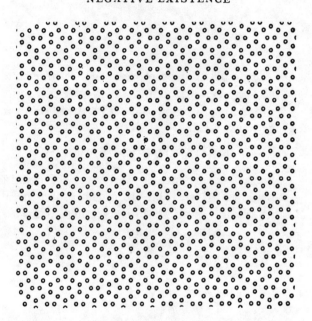

Here Negative Existence is represented by an
infinite number of dots distributed equally
throughout infinity.

This is a further enlargement of
NEGATIVE EXISTENCE

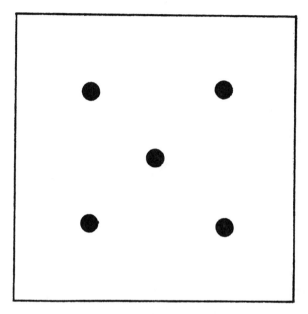

Each dot can now be seen as a discrete individual. The dots begin to take on the quality
of Positive Existence with respect to the background void representing Negative Existence.

The dot represents the Self
or 'I' of the Creator.

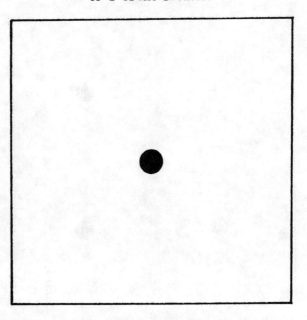

The dot indicates an infinitely small point
which, as yet, has no dimensions.
The point is invisible while its existence is indicated with a dot.
The point represents the Creator in the state
called EHEIEH (ee-eye-ah) which means 'I shall
be'. The Creator steps out of Negative Existence into Positive Existence in the act of becoming an individual.
The Creator is now finite with respect to the
infinity of Negative Existence. He is at the
same time infinite with respect to Positive
Existence of which He is the source.

A dot is infinite potential.
A Creator is infinite ability.

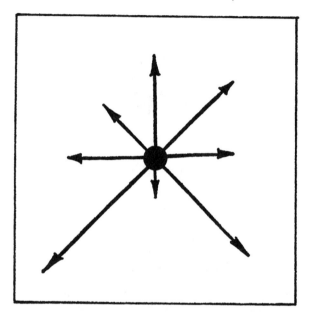

A dot can move any distance in any direction.
A dot represents infinite potential.
As a dot, the Creator is in the act of becoming (EHEIEH).
As a moving dot, the Creator is in the act
of creating.
In the act of creating, the Creator is in the state
called JEHOVAH which means essence of being.
As the Creator, He is infinite ability in action.
Action is the essence of being.
All graphic forms are created by the path of a dot.
All manifest existence is created by the
activity of the Creator.

The Activity of the Creator

Stage I   Non-dimensionality

The dot is replaced with a dotted circle indicating the existence of an infinitely small point at its center.

This is the Self of the Creator in the state of Eheieh, the state of becoming.

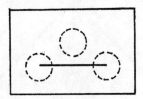

Stage II   One dimension

The movement of the dot in one direction creates a line. A line is the path of a dot between two points.

This is the Self of the Creator moving between the state of Jehovah (doing) and the state of relating (Jehovah Elohim). The line indicates the primal intentionality of the Creator.

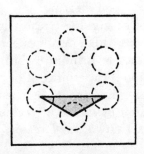

Stage III   Two dimensions

The movement of a dot in two directions creates a plane. A plane is the path of a dot between three points.

This is the Self of the Creator moving between three states which are the reflection of the first three states on a lower level. Here the prime intentionality is split into two directions forming the polarity of the creative and receptive. The third state is the balance point between the two. The balance point falls directly below the state of Eheieh on the center line. This indicates the Self of the Creator in a state in which He is subject to the polarity He has created.

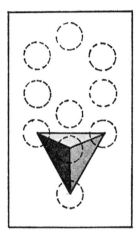

Stage IV   Three dimensions

The movement of a dot in three directions creates a solid. A solid is the path of a dot between four or more points.

The four points represent a synthesis of all the previous states stabilized in three-dimensional existence. The Self of the Creator is stabilized in a state which, at the apex of a pyramid, balances the polarities of male-female and spirit-matter at its base. The pyramid represents the universe created by the activity of the Creator who now dwells within it.

The graphic geometrical progression shows how a dot of infinite potential, through its activity, describes an increasingly finite demonstration of its potential. In the same way, the Creator is infinite ability while His creation is an increasingly finite demonstration of that ability.

This is the 'I' of the Creator.

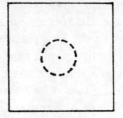

This is the Creator's body.

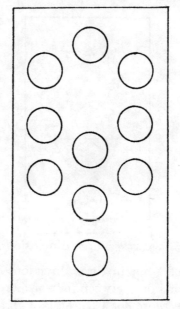

The structure shown above is called the 'Tree of Life'. The Hebrew words which are translated to read 'Tree of Life' mean 'Concept of Being', or what philosophers call ontology. Each of the ten circles is called a Sephira (Sephiroth in the plural). They are said to emanate from the Creator's being as form can be said to emanate from the dot.

Both the Creator and the dot are everywhere in their creations since whatever they create is composed of their nature. The Tree of Life is the archetypal pattern through which being becomes form.

The Tree of Life

The Tree of Life is the symbolic basis of an ancient and vast metaphysical system known as the Qabalah. The Qabalah is a guide to the inner truths which underlie the outer form of the Jewish and Christian religions. With respect to the Absolute, all religious dogmas and philosophies are limited viewpoints. The Symbolic Qabalah offers a more direct means of apprehending the Absolute by helping the seeker to transcend all viewpoints through the use of universal symbols.

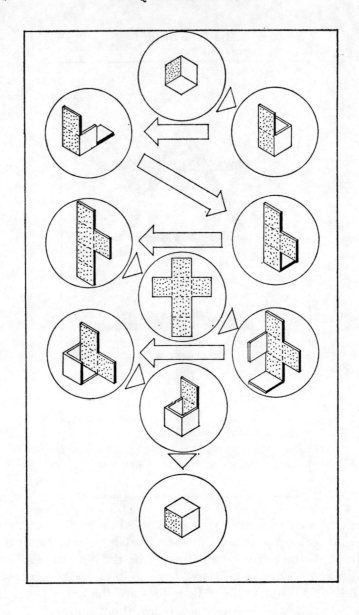

The Unfolding of Man

The Tree of Life describes the unfolding transition from God to Man. The diagram on the opposite page shows God (represented as a cube). God, the 'I shall be', occupies the first position at the top of the diagram. Man, 'the image and likeness of God', occupies the last position at the bottom of the diagram. In the sixth position, half way between God and Man, is the state of consciousness called 'Christ', symbolized by the cross.

The cube at the top is like a cardboard box. Its surface represents consciousness of divinity. As it is shown we can only see three of its six surfaces. As the box unfolds (follow the arrows), all six surfaces are exposed in the cross. The cross then folds back into a box but this time the outer surface is inside the box. In the tenth position, the box whose surface has been reversed represents consciousness of the material world, containing consciousness of divinity hidden within.

In Qabalah, 'Christ' is not seen as a personage. Christ is a state of consciousness which was personified by many individuals in history, including the man Jesus. It is a state of consciousness in which spirituality and materialism, consciousness of self and consciousness of others, and the inner divinity and outer personality are in perfect balance. The attainment of this state of consciousness is the objective of studying the Qabalah.

The Lord's Prayer in the Tree of Life

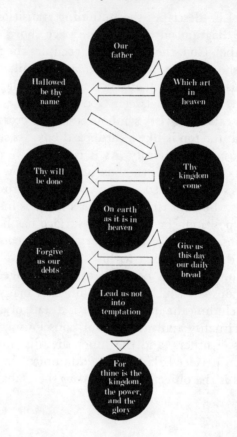

The Lord's Prayer, attributed to Jesus, is used in most, if not all, Christian sects. Its language parallels the older Jewish prayer called the Kadish. The prayer, by its very construction, divides itself into ten separate statements. These ten statements correspond in many ways to the ten Sephiroth of the Tree of Life. Assuming that Jesus was the author, this suggests that he was familiar with Qabalistic symbolism.[1]

The Sephiroth

Each Sephira has a title and a number indicating its sequence of creation.

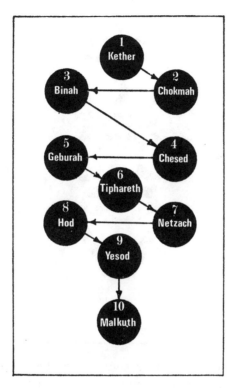

1² Kether   Crown
2 Chokmah   Wisdom
3 Binah   Understanding
4 Chesed   Mercy
5 Geburah   Strength
6 Tiphareth Beauty
7 Netzach   Victory
8 Hod   Splendor/or Glory
9 Yesod   Foundation
10 Malkuth   Kingdom

The Paths

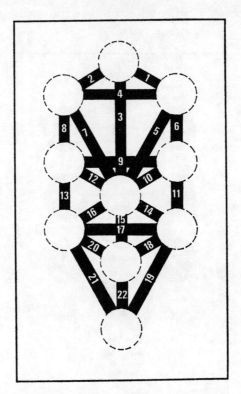

There are twenty-two paths connecting the Sephiroth of the Tree of Life. Each path (column one, opposite) corresponds with one of the twenty-two Hebrew letters[3] (column two), one of the twenty-two astrological correspondences[4] (column three), and one of the twenty-two major arcana-images containing mysteries – of the Tarot (column four for the number of the card and column five for its title).

1	*aleph*	Uranus	0	The Fool
2	*bayt*	Mercury	1	The Magician
3	*ghimmel*	Moon	2	The High Priestess
4	*dallet*	Venus	3	The Empress
5	*hay*	Aries	4	The Emperor
6	*vav*	Taurus	5	The Hierophant
7	*zayn*	Gemini	6	The Lovers
8	*chayt*	Cancer	7	The Chariot
9	*tayt*	Leo	8	Strength
10	*yod*	Virgo	9	The Hermit
11	*khaf*	Jupiter	10	The Wheel of Fortune
12	*lammed*	Libra	11	Justice
13	*mem*	Neptune	12	The Hanged Man
14	*noon*	Scorpio	13	Death
15	*sammekh*	Sagittarius	14	Temperance
16	*ayn*	Capricorn	15	The Devil
17	*phay*	Mars	16	The Tower
18	*tsadde*	Aquarius	17	The Star
19	*qof*	Pisces	18	The Moon
20	*raysh*	Sun	19	The Sun
21	*sheen*	Pluto	20	The Judgement
22	*tav*	Saturn	21	The World

The Seven Planes of Existence

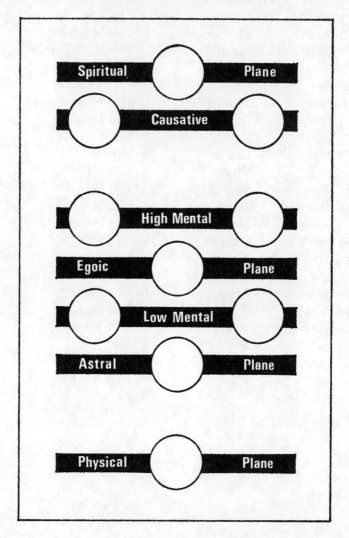

By drawing lines horizontally through each Sephira or pair of Sephiroth, the seven levels of existence are indicated. These are the seven heavens which can be found in many religious and theosophic teachings.[5]

The Pillars of Duality

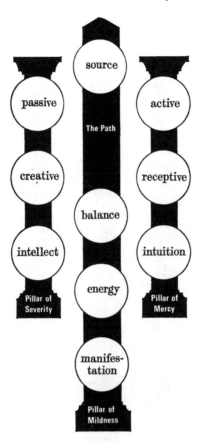

The Tree of Life relates infinite to finite, microcosmic to macro-cosmic, inner to outer, thesis to antithesis, attitude to its opposite attitude, and provides a scale on which to weigh meaning and consequence. It is a way of differentiating between apparent similarities, reconciling apparent contradictions, and synthesizing philosophies.

Through the use of the Tree of Life one can bring into awareness previously unconscious or inconceivable ideas. The development of these primary abilities is measured as intelligence.

The Behind of Appearances

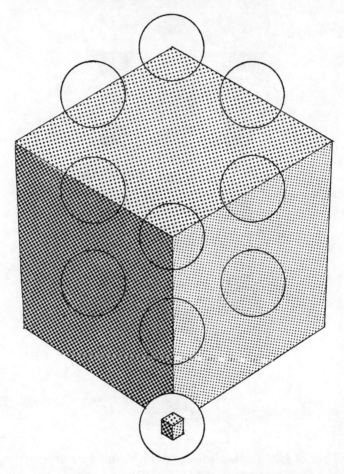

The Tree of Life seeks to describe the reality which underlies all appearances. The cube in the tenth Sephira represents the outer manifestation of the nine previous Sephiroth acting together as a unity.

The Seven Rays

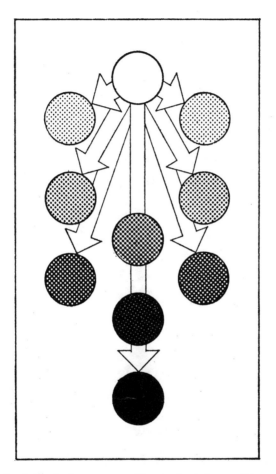

The first Sephira is the source. By analogy it can be represented as white light. If the white light of the first Sephira is projected through the other nine Sephiroth it is divided into its component colors and shades just as light is refracted by a prism. The Theosophists call this phenomenon the seven rays of creation.

The Seven Chakras

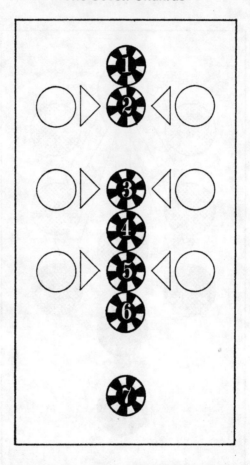

A *chakra* is an energy center in the body. When the polarities symbolized by the three pairs of opposites (to the left and right of the center column) are in balance the *chakra* beween them will open. A *chakra* which is opened affords the individual inner powers of perception and creativity. The first *chakra*, at the top of the diagram, is called the Crown Chakra. Moving down the diagram are The Third Eye (2), Throat Chakra (3), Heart Chakra (4), Solar Plexus Chakra (5), Belly Chakra or Hara (6), and the Base Chakra (7).

Three-Acting-As-One

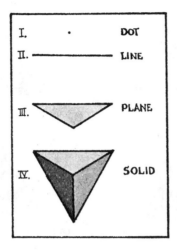

At the beginning of this chapter it was shown how the Tree of Life was generated out of a four stage geometric progression. In the progression, the three qualities of dot, line, and plane came together to produce the solid in the fourth stage. All apparently static things can be described as processes. All processes can be described in terms of three qualities acting together to produce a fourth.

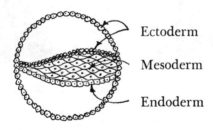

Ectoderm

Mesoderm

Endoderm

THE EMBRYONIC DISK

The human body grows out of an embryo composed of three kinds of cells.

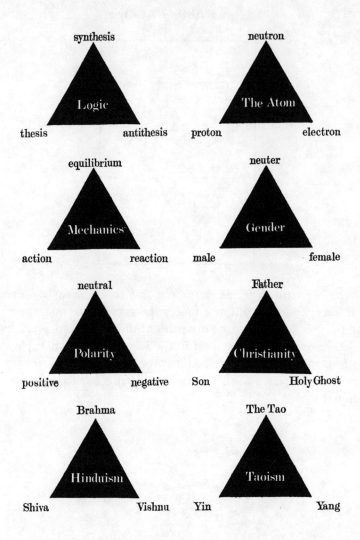

The Tetragrammaton: The Four-fold Process Called God

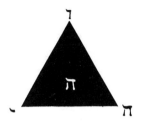

The trinity-acting-as-one in the Qabalah is called the Tetra-grammaton. Its four letters spell the inexpressible name of God. Although it is sometimes translated as Jehovah, it is not really a name but a formula describing a universal process.

 The first letter, *yod,* is the simplest in construction of all the Hebrew letters. It is the fundamental unit by which the other letters are formed. It symbolizes a flame. It is male, active, and creative. It is the principle of FORCE.

 The second letter, *hay,* is female, passive, and acts as the container or formative principle with respect to *yod. Hay* is the principle of PATTERN.

 The third letter, *vav,* is the activity of *yod* (force) moving through the pattern of *hay. Vav* is the principle of ACTIVITY.

 Hay is repeated as the fourth letter of the Tetra-grammaton. Here it indicates a pattern or structure which is the resultant of the first three letters acting-as-one. The second *hay* indicates manifestation or FORM.

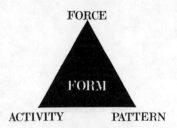

Four general qualities can be abstracted from all these. The qualities are Force, Pattern, Activity, and Form.

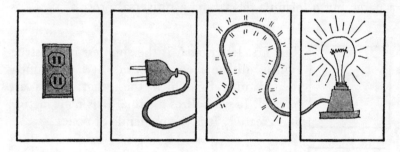

A simple example of the Tetragrammaton (three-acting-as-one) is an electric circuit. The FORCE (electricity) moves through a PATTERN (wiring) causing an ACTIVITY (current flowing) which results in the FORM (the work done by the whole system, in this case the production of light).

The four aspects of the Tetragrammaton are symbolized by the four elements – fire, water, air, and earth; the four suits of the minor arcana of the tarot – scepters, cups, coins, and swords, from which the modern playing card suits of clubs, hearts, diamonds, and spades are derived. In astrology they correspond to the four fixed signs of the zodiac which symbolize the four corners of the universe.[6]

The Tree As Microcosm

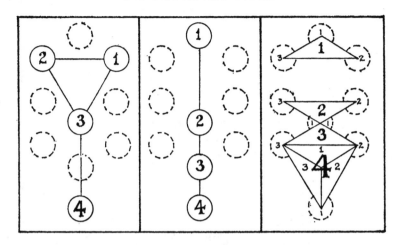

The Tetragrammaton can be applied to the relationship between Sephiroth. Here it is applied on a microcosmic scale.

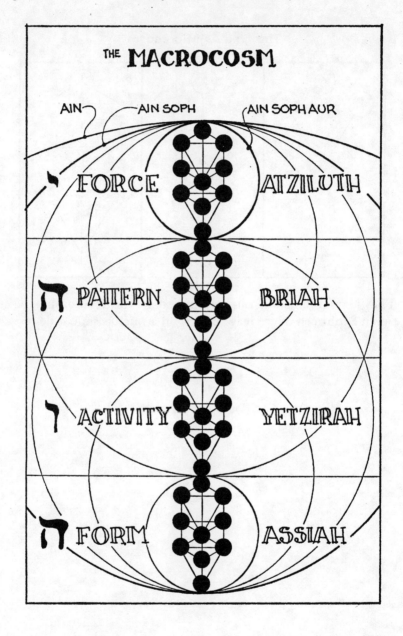

The Four Worlds of The Macrocosm

Four Qabalistic worlds, each containing a Tree of Life, symbolize the nature of the whole of Positive Existence (the Macrocosm). Each world has a title and each Sephira within that world is assigned a name.

ATZILUTH is the first world arising out of Negative Existence. Its title is 'The Boundless World of Divine Names'. Each Sephira in this world is assigned one of the Hebrew names for what is translated in English as 'God'.

BRIAH, the second world, emanates from the tenth Sephira in Briah. It is 'The Hierarchical World of Formations'. Each Sephira is named after an angelic order or power.

YETZIRAH, the third world, emanates from the tenth Sephira in Atziluth. It is the 'Archangelic World of Creations'. Each Sephira is named after an archangel.

ASSIAH is the fourth world. It is 'The Elemental World of Substances'. Each Sephira is given an astrological correspondence. The tenth Sephira in Assiah is 'The Sphere of the Four Elements'. The four elements – fire, water, air and earth – refer back to the four aspects of the Tetragrammaton. This suggests that the whole of the Macrocosm is within the lowest Sephira on the lowest tree (the Microcosm).

A Peek at God

The Qabalistic literature seems to reinforce the still popular idea that a vast separation exists between Man and God. The older the literature is, the more it tends to emphasize the difference between them: 'Woe be to him who compares Him (God) to his own attributes or still worse with the son of Man whose foundation is in the dust, who vanishes and is no more.'

In order to describe an essential whole, the Qabalah, like all systems of classification, must describe the parts of the whole. Unfortunately, until the whole is fully described and put back together, the system, by its very nature, reinforces the temporary illusion of separateness.

The essence of the whole is a four letter name. It is written that this name is the key to understanding all that humanity can comprehend concerning the nature of the whole of reality. Look carefully at the name itself. It suggests what God might look like.

2
A Brief Summary of the Qabalah

Qabalah is a system of religious philosophy. It contains within it the inner teachings and mystical significance of both the Jewish and Christian religions.

Qabalah (spelled variously Cabala, Kabalah, etc., with the accent on the first syllable) comes from the Hebrew verb *qabal* which means both 'to receive' and 'to reveal'. The word Revelation, the title of the last book of the Bible, although derived from the Greek, has the same meaning. The initial letters of Qabalah in Hebrew mean 'the grace of God'. The Qabalah is also referred to as 'The Secret Wisdom' since it was handed down by tradition 'through the initiated and is indicated in the Hebrew scriptures by signs which are hidden to all but the initiated.'

Historical Note

No one seems to know exactly how old the Qabalah is but it is generally acknowledged that it antedates the Old Testament of the Bible at least in its oral tradition. There are two basic stories which can be found in the literature[8] concerning the source of Qabalah:

1. God taught the mysteries of the Qabalah to a select band of angels before the fall of Man. The angels then instructed Adam so that through an understanding of its principles he might ascend to heaven again. The Qabalah was then passed orally from generation to generation with the help of the angels.

2. Moses ascended Mt. Sinai three times. Each time he sat in the presence of God for forty days. The first time he received the written law, the second time he received the soul of the law, the third time he received the soul of the soul of the law which is the Qabalah and its mysteries. Moses then covertly laid down

the sacred mysteries in the first five books of the Bible (called the Pentateuch.)

The classical Qabalah can be divided into five parts: The Oral Tradition, The Written Qabalah, The Literal or Cryptic Qabalah, The Symbolic Qabalah and The Practical Qabalah.

The Oral Tradition

The oral tradition refers to the practice of handing down the secrets of Qabalah from father to son or teacher to student verbally. There existed, and exist now, schools and secret orders which preserve this tradition. The oral tradition dates back to pre-history.

Although the Qabalah is a cornerstone of both the Jewish and Christian religions, you will not find it spoken of, either in contemporary churches or synagogues. The overwhelming majority of today's theologians either have no knowledge of it or only have a vague academic idea of its content. Many consider the Qabalah to be pure superstition. Still others consider it to be evil and many forbid their members even to read about it.

In the classical Jewish tradition, in those sects (usually Hasidic) which teach Qabalah, the man must be over forty years old, have raised a family, and have a thorough knowledge of the outer scriptural teachings.

Without any disrespect intended, the author does not qualify on any of these points.

The Written Qabalah

The written Qabalah consists of either the texts of attempts to write down the oral teachings or commentaries on what has already been written. The vast amount of commentaries available today are based on the four works which are said to be the sources of the written Qabalah: The Sepher Yetzirah, known as 'The Book of Formation', is attributed to Rabbi Akiba (around A.D. 120); The Sepher Ha Zohar, called 'The Book of Splendour', by Simeon Ben Jochai (A.D. 160); The Commentaries on the Ten Sephiros, by Rabbi Ezra (12th century); and the Book of Revelation in the Bible.

Legend has it that the secret doctrines of Israel existed since the beginning of the world but Rabbi Simeon was the first to write it down. 1200 years later they were discovered and published by Moses De Lyon as the Zohar. Some authorities dispute the authenticity of the Zohar and claim that Moses De Lyon is himself the author (A.D. 1305).

At present there are hundreds of works about the Qabalah. Almost all of them refer back to one of these original documents and then interpret them according to one viewpoint or another.

The following is a brief abstract of the information contained in these volumes and should in no way be considered complete.

The Qabalah seeks to explain the transition from the infinite to the finite, the procedure from the absolute to the relative, the relationship between matter and intelligence, the influence of intelligence on matter, and the relationship between the Creator and the creation.

The major doctrines of the Qabalah seek to elucidate the nature of the Supreme Being, the cosmological structure of the universe, the creation of angels and man, the destiny of the universe, and the importance and inner meaning of revealed law (the scriptures).

In the literature, God is called Ayn Soph, which means endless and boundless. He is absolute unity. There is nothing without Him and He is in everything. The Ayn Soph cannot be comprehended through the intellect nor can He be represented in words. As far as our minds are concerned, He does not exist since, in the realm of the mind, what cannot be comprehended does not exist. In order to make His existence perceptible, the Ayn Soph had to become active and creative. But the Ayn Soph cannot create directly for He has no will, intention, desire, thought, language, or action since all of these attributes are finite and limited while the Ayn Soph is limitless and infinite. The Ayn Soph cannot produce anything which is unlike Himself, boundless and perfect.

Yet the universal order of things suggests that the world is not a child of chance but is of intelligent design. Therefore the Ayn Soph is viewed as the *indirect* creator of the world. The medium by which the Ayn Soph made His existence known in the created world are the ten Sephiroth (Sephira, in the singular, meaning light, emanation or intelligence) which emanated from the Boundless One.

In archaic language, the Qabalistic text sets forth the generation of the Qabalistic cosmology:

'The Aged of Aged, the Unknown of the Unknown has a form and yet has no form. He has a form whereby the universe is preserved, and yet has no form, because He cannot be comprehended. When He first assumed form (of the first Sephira), He caused nine splendid lights to emanate from it, which, shining through it, diffused a bright light in all directions. Imagine an elevated light sending forth its light in all directions. Now if we approach it to examine the rays, we understand no more than that they emanate from the said light. So is the Holy Aged an absolute light, but in Himself concealed and incomprehensible. We can only comprehend Him through those luminous emanations which are partly visible and partly concealed. These constitute the sacred name of God.[7] At first, the Ayn Soph sent forth from His infinite light one spiritual substance or intelligence. The first Sephira is called the Crown and is expressed in the Bible by the divine name Ehejah (or Eheieh pronounced ee-eye-ah), or 'I AM', because it is absolute being and represents the infinite as distinct from the finite. The first Sephira contains the other nine and gave rise to them in order.'

To paraphrase the Sepher Yetzirah, 'God engraved His holy name and formed and created the universe in thirty-two mysterious sequences, by numbers, letters, and sounds which are in Him. Ten Sephiroth and twenty-two letters (the Hebrew alphabet) are the foundation of all things. The ten numbers are analogous to the ten fingers and ten toes; five over against five. In the center between them is the covenant with the Only One God. Ten are the numbers (of the Sephiroth) out of nothing; ten, not nine; ten, not eleven. Comprehend this wisdom, understand this knowledge, and be wise. Enquire into the mystery and ponder it. Examine all things by means of the ten Sephiroth, restore the world to its Creator and lead the Creator back to His throne again. He is the only formator and beside Him there is no other. His attributes are ten and are without limit.

'The appearance of the ten spheres (Sephiroth) out of nothing is as a flash of lightning and they are without beginning or end. The word of God is in them when they go forth and when they return. They run by His order and prostrate themselves before His throne.

'The ten Sephiroth have their end linked to their beginning and their beginning linked to their end, conjoined as the flame is to the live coal, for the Lord is Superlatively One and to Him there is no second.

'Concerning the number of the spheres out of existence out of nothing, seal up your lips and guard your heart as you consider them, and if your mouth opens for utterances and your heart turns toward thought, control them, returning to silence. So it is written "And the living creatures ran and returned" (Ezekiel 14). And on this wise was the covenant made with us.'

The Sepher Yetzirah relates the letters of the Hebrew alphabet to their symbols. It describes the twenty-two letters as being based on the three fundamental letters: *aleph*, which is the symbol for air, *sheen*, which is the symbol for fire, and *mem*, which is water. It assigns to each of the seven double letters a planet and to each of the remaining twelve simple letters it assigns a sign of the zodiac. The Sepher Yetzirah then continues with the following admonition: 'God also set the opposites against each other; the good against the evil and the evil against the good.' Of the trinity (the first three letters and the first three Sephiroth) it says: 'There are three, of which each stands by itself: one is in the affirmative; one is negative; and the third equilibrates them.

'Over all these rule God, the faithful king, from His holy habitation in all eternity. God is one above three, three are above seven, seven are above twelve, yet all are linked together.

'There are twenty-two letters by which the I AM, the Lord God of Hosts, Almighty and Eternal, designed and created, by the three Sepherim (numbers, letter, and sounds), His universe, and formed by them all creatures and all those things which are yet to come.'

The Literal Qabalah

The Literal Qabalah is concerned with the codification of information in scripture, including both the Old and New Testaments of the Bible. The idea that scripture is a codified body of knowledge is either unknown to, or disbelieved by, most theologians, let alone the average Jew or Christian. This fact accounts for the apparently illogical and somewhat strange passages which appear in all modern language translations of the Bible.

The original Hebrew text had no vowels, all the letters are consonants. The vowel sounds were added later with the use of dots and punctuation to indicate the modern pronunciation. In addition, the original scriptural scrolls did not have spaces between the words as we have in modern writing so the translators must have decided for themselves when a word ended and a new one began.

Each letter of the Hebrew alphabet is not only a letter but is, at the same time, a number. There was no other number system besides the alphabet used in scripture. The letters each have two numbers associated with them: the number associated with its sequence in the alphabet, and a numerical value which is different from the numerical sequence after the tenth letter (the eleventh letter is valued at 20).

Each letter is also a word when spelled out in full[9] representing an object (*aleph* means ox). In addition each letter stands for an archetypal idea (*aleph* = force) which may or may not be the same idea contained in the word which spells out the letter. Since the letters themselves are a form of shorthand, each a simplified picture, each represents an archetypal image which corresponds to the twenty-two major cards of the tarot (sometimes ignorantly referred to as 'fortune telling cards').

Each Hebrew letter has a place on the structure called the Tree of Life, connecting two of the Sephiroth with a line which is called a path or channel (See Chapter One, p. 26). A letter's position on the tree of the ten Sephiroth indicates a relationship between the aspects of God that it connects. Each letter also is assigned either an element, a planet, or an astrological correspondence. (See p. 27)

Briefly, here are some of the methods by which scripture has been codified:

Carlos Suarès describes a way of reading Hebrew code directly or intuitively[10]. It is required that the student of this method commit to memory the archetypal ideas and feelings contained within each of the letters. Then he is able to read the letters as if they were part of an equation and not as if they are parts of words. The reader in this way allows each letter to evoke a feeling which when connected to the other letter-feelings tells an intuitive story.

A method of codification called Gematria substitutes the corresponding numerical value for each letter of a word or phrase. Another word or phrase with the same numerical value is substituted for the original. Thus words and phrases are substituted for others to yield either different meanings or complementary insights into the meanings of the original phrase.

In another method of codification, called Notaricon, every letter in a word is taken as the initial or abbreviation of another word. A variation of this method is to take the first and last letters of a word and compose a new word from them.

Another method, called Temurah, is used in which words or phrases which are suspected of having a hidden meaning are arranged on a grid like an anagram or crossword puzzle. The letters can then be read backwards as well as forwards, up as well as down, and diagonally as well.

Another system splits the alphabet in half. The second half of the alphabet is then placed under the first half. Then the top letters are substituted for the bottom letters and vice versa.

As if all this isn't complicated enough, two or more codification methods are combined so that one word of scripture can be made to yield paragraphs of information. Since this can be a very subjective practice, it is not possible to prove that the meanings derived through the use of these codes are in fact the meanings intended by the original authors. But this statement holds true for the many different translations and interpretations which make up the dogma of established religions in the West.

In the Bible there are eleven Hebrew names, all of which

are translated into English as God.* Each of these names refers
to different aspects of God – or defines God differently – all of
which are lost in translation. Some Qabalists say that all the
names in the Bible refer to states of consciousness and that all
the place names refer to qualities or conditions or consciousness.
For example, Abraham refers to the state of consciousness we
call faith; Bethlehem refers to the dwelling place of the divine
forces within each one of us.

In the following chapter entitled 'The Creative Law', the use
of these codes comprising the Literal Qabalah are utilized to
reveal the inner meaning of scripture.

The Symbolic Qabalah

The Symbolic Qabalah arises out of and is described by the
Written Qabalah. It consists basically of two aspects: the Tetragrammaton – the four letter formula or 'Name' of God – and the
diagram showing the arrangement of the Sephiroth, the Tree of
Life.

The Tetragrammaton will be discussed in more detail in the
chapter on the Creative Law. (See also Chapter One p. 35)

The Tree of Life graphically represents the wisdom of the
Qabalistic teachings. The diagram is an object of meditation for
the student who becomes an active participant in the wisdom
derived through its use.

The Tree of Life is a geometric arrangement of the names,
symbols, numbers and letters referred to in the Written Qabalah. It allows the student to see the vast amount of information
contained in the Qabalah integrated in one symbol. It shows
how all the aspects of Qabalah relate to one another. It is the
means by which the student integrates the wisdom into his own
mind.

The Tree of Life diagram consists of ten spheres or Sephiroth,
each of which denotes an aspect of God and a basic principle

* The eleven Names of God in the Bible do not correspond exactly to the
ten Names of God in the Qabalistic World of Atziluth. The colloquial name
Jehovah, however, has two aspects, since it refers also to the Tetragrammaton,
which can be considered as the eleventh name.

upon which the universe is built. As we have seen, connecting the Sephiroth are twenty-two paths or channels, each corresponding to one of the Hebrew letters.

The first substance or intelligence that God emanates from Negative Existence, as the written Qabalah tells us, is called the Crown which is the title of the first Sephira in the Tree of Life and is the beginning of Positive Existence. Thus, the Tree of Life is a symbolic description of Positive Existence, in which God is the indirect creator of the universe.

The following are brief summaries of what the literature tells us about each of the ten Sephiroth:

The first Sephira is Kether, the Crown, and is attributed the Yetziric appellation Hidden Intelligence. It is the result of the Ayn Soph Aur becoming centered or one-pointed. From this state the all-pervading light becomes focussed, and becomes the source of all succeeding ideation and manifestation.

The second Sephira is Chokmah,* Wisdom, and is called Illuminating Intelligence. It is associated with maleness – the active, positive principle, and it also called Abba, the great father. The transition from the first Sephira to the second takes place as the Ayn Soph Aur, still infinite, creates a reflection of itself, which makes the first duality. Chokmah, as the reflection, then takes on the aspect of the Creator in the first step from the infinite to the finite.

The third Sephira is Binah, Understanding, also known as the Sanctifying Intelligence. Its aspects are feminine, receptive, negative, and it is also known as Aima, the great mother. It represents the essence of substance, while Chokmah represents the essence of Consciousness. It is the underlying objective reality behind the whole of existence.

The first three Sephiroth are called the Supernals. They are separated from the following seven Sephiroth called the Inferiors, by the Abyss. The Abyss is a metaphysical gap which separates the conceivable from the inconceivable. The Supernal Triangle, formed by the first three Sephiroth, is ideal with respect to the actuality of the Inferiors. The gap indicates that

* 'Ch' is pronounced as a guttural H.

normal intellection must give way to a more direct means of apprehension before the Supernals can be perceived.

The fourth Sephira is Chesed, Mercy, and it is termed the Recepticular Intelligence. It is the first of the seven Inferior Sephiroth, which are also called the potencies of Construction. Like Chokmah, it has male, active, positive attributes but they are acting on a lower level. The triangle formed by the second three Sephiroth are said to be a reflection of the first three, just as Chokmah is a reflection of Kether.

The fifth Sephira is Geburah, Severity, and it is called the Radical Intelligence. Like Binah on a lower level of existence, it is feminine, receptive and negative in nature. Unlike Binah, it is attributed with the qualities of strength, power, and force.

The sixth Sephira is Tiphareth, Beauty, and it is known as the Mediating Intelligence. Beauty, harmony, and equilibrium are attributed to it and it indicates, by its position in the center of the Tree, the activity of Kether within the realm of form. Considering Chokmah as father, Binah as mother, then Tiphareth is the son.

The seventh Sephira is Netzach, Victory, and it is the Occult Intelligence. It is a masculine sphere, attributed with the qualities of love and the generative forces in nature.

The eighth Sephira is Hod, Glory, and it is called the Absolute or Perfect Intelligence. This feminine sphere is concerned with intellectual nature and inventivenss.

The ninth Sephira is Yesod, Foundation, the Pure or Clear Intelligence. It sits at the center of the Tree below Tiphareth and is considered as representing the subtle basis of the physical world. It indicates the ebb and flow of the world's forces and is associated with the astral plane.

The tenth Sephira is Malkuth, Kingdom, and it is the Resplendent Intelligence. It represents matter in its entirety and is therefore the Tree of Life's equivalent to physical matter. This sphere contains all the others and is the result of the activity of the previous nine Sephiroth. It is written 'Kether is in Malkuth, Malkuth is in Kether, though after a different manner.'

The Practical Qabalah

The Practical Qabalah includes any utilization of the various aspects of Qabalah to change one's consciousness or the way one lives.

The application of the concepts found in Qabalah to one's way of seeing life is the primary function of practical Qabalah. The process entails the systematic use of its symbolism to test all assumptions concerning the nature of the self, life and others. It is a process of bringing reason and logic to bear on what has previously been an untested belief.

The early literature implores the seeker to examine all things by means of the ten Sephiroth. The Sephiroth are those basic aspects of God (seen as the whole of creation) which are available to conceptual, rational thought. The student of Qabalah has at his finger tips a decimal filing system in which to locate all his psychological and philosophical ideas. To do so, he must clarify his thoughts about all the apparent dichotomies such as good and evil, male and female, and inner and outer experience. The process is one of expanding mentality to encompass an ever-widening view of reality. Consciousness is expanded in the process.

This leads the seeker to realize that he can rely more and more on his own ability to know truth internally. He thus finds that he has broken through the bounds of normal rational thought into the deeper realm of mystical experience. Mystical experiences are simply more direct ways of knowing things than rational thought alone affords. Since the mystical or more direct way of knowing truth is attained through the process of clearing the mind of fixed attitudes, he can test every mystical insight against the rationally built conception of reality that the Qabalah has given him. He finds that what he once would have called mystical is really a purer form of rationality.

Magic or Hermetics is another aspect of the practical Qabalah. On the surface, ceremonial magic is concerned with the contacting of beings outside the physical world such as angels, powers or elementals. Once contacted, the spirits are asked to perform some service for the practitioner or yield some information. Actually, the inner purpose of the ceremony is to develop the ability to concentrate the will. It is a form of meditation. Ceremonies are also used to mark the change from one stage of personal growth to another. This was the original intent of the ceremonies now used in many of the churches of the world.

Astrology, Alchemy and Tarot are also allied to the practical Qabalah. Many organizations such as the Rosicrucians and the Masons owe their ceremonies and teachings to the Qabalah.

Beneath all the symbolism and ceremony of the various schools of practical Qabalah, including the modern church and synagogue practices, there is a basic process – the process by which one contacts Truth. It is the same principle by which intentionality becomes manifest.

In the following chapter, entitled The Creative Law, various aspects of Qabalah will be applied to scripture to demonstrate this basic process.

3
The Creative Law,
The Principle of Creativity

Introduction

The Creative Law, as it is presented here, was formulated by Samuel Bousky of Redwood City, California. He is a research physicist specializing in the application of laser technology to high density data recording systems. (The Symbolic Qabalah can be described as a metaphysical, high density data recording system.) He says that decoding scripture with the use of the Qabalistic code is his hobby.

In a statement as to how he discovered it, Sam says: 'I didn't hear voices or have any visions; nor did I read it in a book. I put it together like a jigsaw puzzle, only, for me, it was more difficult since I didn't recognize the pieces when I first saw them.'

I think it is important to point out that Sam does not consider himself to be a religious man but a man of science. He had no interest in the Bible before he heard about some of its mysteries from the late Neville Goddard.

Sam discovered – or, more accurately, rediscovered – it, by applying the codification systems of the Literal and Symbolic Qabalah to the Hebrew text of the Bible. Although the source of this material is the Bible, he does not claim (nor do I) that the Creative Law should be believed simply because the Bible is its source. Belief or faith in something should be used as a hypothesis is used in science – a temporary model for, or method of, discovering what is actually true or useful. It is not necessarily the truth itself.

In 1969, Sam gave two weekend seminars on the Creative Law for me and my associates at Bridge Mountain Foundation, a small residential growth center in Ben Lomond, California. Since then many of those present, including myself, have applied its principles successfully to various aspects of our lives.

In using the Creative Law, I have concluded that it is the method by which each human being creates and sustains his or her thoughts, feelings, and behavior. It is how we program our minds with attitudes, assumptions, and beliefs. It is how we create mental images of ourselves called egos. It is how we participate in socially created systems, such as the existing religious, economic, and political systems. It is the way we create the circumstances of our lives, and the events which we either call accident or assign to fate.

It is also a law not unlike the laws of gravity and electromagnetism. It is in operation in our lives whether or not we are conscious of its existence, and whether or not we believe it to to be good or bad.

Before we knew about the many physical laws that affect us we were more or less subject to them. Now that we understand them we have gained the ability to use them. As a result, our ability to change things for what we consider to be the better has increased a thousand-fold.

For most of us the principle called the Creative Law is deeply subconscious. Nevertheless, it is active in the lives of all of us. Such laws do not have a built-in morality. They function in directions both for and against us. If we wish to utilize a law to improve our circumstance then we must first make it conscious to ourselves and understand its principles.

This law, unlike the laws of physics, operates not only in the physical world but also in the spiritual and psychological worlds. It therefore is harder to pin down in laboratory situations and will probably not be discovered by science for quite some time, if ever. There is, then, no proof that the Creative Law exists nor that it functions in the ways that are described here. But scientists have no proof that gravity and electricity exist as they conceive them; nor do they know exactly what they are. Science has simply learned to utilize them and describe their functions.

The way that scientists prove the existence of some law or principle is by showing that other scientists in a different laboratory can use the law and get the same results. This is the way you will prove to yourself the existence of the Creative Law – in the laboratory of your own life.

The following section explains the methods that Samuel Bousky has used to uncover the Creative Law. In the process of its description, he gives many examples of the application of the Literal and Symbolic Qabalah to scripture. The information is taken from a series of taped lectures Sam gave at Finca La Follenca, a residential growth center in the south of Spain, in the spring of 1972.

At the beginning of the lectures, Sam points out that each one of us is a creative being. By this he means that we are creative far beyond the usual connotation of that word. We are not only creative in the artistic or constructive sense but we are able to change basic things in our personal and interpersonal lives. Again, there is no way to prove this fact. It can only be proved by each person who tries it and finds that it works for him in his daily life.

The Four Levels of Comprehension in the Bible

As I have mentioned, Samuel Bousky uncovered the Creative Law (or principle) by applying the Literal and Symbolic aspects of Qabalah to the Hebrew text of the Bible*. In order to understand the Creative Law and appreciate its significance, the way in which it was unearthed should be understood.

The Bible is written on four levels of comprehension – the historical, allegorical, cryptic, and Qabalistic levels.

The Historical Level

The historical level of the Bible is a narrative of the events which took place in the lives of the Jewish and Christian peoples over a period of some 4,000 years.

The Allegorical Level

The allegorical level of the Bible is a hidden description of a step by step process of personal spiritual evolution. To para-

---

*In addition to Qabalistic references Sam uses some definitions and meanings obtained from *The Unity Dictionary*[11] and *Strong's Exhaustive Concordance*.[12]

phrase Sam's statements, he says that the whole allegorical story of the Bible is the development from Adam to Christ of each individual human being. Adam is prototype Man, the animal nature. Christ is the God-Man, the divine nature. The Bible is a detailed story of that growth, its pitfalls, the directions it takes, and the guidance needed when taking the journey.

All the names in the Bible, especially those of the Old Testament, are codified personal names representing stages of consciousness. All the places in the Bible are conditions under which these states of consciousness exist. These states and conditions of consciousness refer to stages that each individual human being goes through in his or her personal growth.

The Bible actually states that there is allegory in it. Paul says: 'For it is written that Abraham had two sons, one by a slave and one by a freed woman. He who was of the slave was born after the flesh. He of the free woman was by promise. These things are an allegory, for these are the two covenants, one from Mt. Sinai and one from Jerusalem.' (Galatians, 4.22-4)

Let us see, then, what the allegory of Abraham and his two sons might also be saying: Abraham means the state of faith or the beginning of spiritual growth; Sarah, the name of the free woman indicates the state of bringing forth divine consciousness; Hagar, the slave woman, means consciousness of the material world or the façade of the personality; Sarah gives birth to Isaac which means the joyous dawning of divine consciousness while Hagar gives birth to Ishmael which is the state of listening inattentively; Sinai refers to some moral code or law enforced on an individual from the outside while Jerusalem, a contraction of two Hebrew words – yara, which means outward flow, and shalom which means peace and harmony – indicates a natural out-flowing of a morality which comes from inner harmony.

By introducing the allegorical meanings, we can see what Paul was probably saying: If you place all your faith in the façade of your materially oriented personality you will attain only a limited awareness, one which requires a moral code to prevent you from being too destructive. If, however, you invest your faith in the bringing forth of your divine nature, you will experience a joyous dawning of divine consciousness within you, one that requires no outside moral code, since you will be in harmony with the universe.

The Cryptic Level

The Cryptic level of the Bible is the secret code or cipher that is hidden within the twenty-two letters of the Hebrew alphabet. The Hebrew alphabet is one in which every letter is also a word. Each letter, as we have said, is also a number and has associated with it an archetypal idea.

The first letter, *aleph*, is an outpouring of breath. It has no sound of its own except when associated with a vowel sound. *Aleph* itself is the expiration or expression referred to in the Bible as The Word (of God). *Aleph* corresponds to A in English, is numerically 1, and, as a word, means ox. The ideas associated with *aleph* are power or strength, insemination or initiation of the creative power.

The second letter, *bayt*, is the number 2 and means house. The idea associated with *bayt* is that which goes on within (us).

Ghimel is the third letter, numerically 3, meaning camel. The idea behind *ghimel* is transition or movement.

Dallet equals 4 and means door. It indicates egress or ingress, or the crossing of a threshold or barrier.

It would take a tremendous number of words to describe fully the archetypal idea behind each letter. These words would tend to be interpreted differently in various cultures and at various times. To preserve their essential meaning, the archetypal ideas contained in the Hebrew letters are presented in pictorial form in the Tarot, using universally understood symbology. Our modern playing cards are derived from the Tarot deck. The fifty-two cards in the modern playing card deck came from what is called the minor arcana (pictures containing mysteries). The major arcana of the Tarot deck consists of an additional twenty-two picture cards. It is in the latter that the archetypal ideas are to be found.

There are over three hundred versions of the classical Tarot. Less than ten of these are readily available today. Since all the decks are slightly different and give different Hebrew letter correspondences, I should mention that Samuel Bousky uses the

Tarot deck published by the Builders of the Adytum, in Los Angeles, California and the meanings given in Paul Case's book.[4]

The following is an example of how the Tarot is substituted for the corresponding Hebrew letters to expose a greater understanding of their meaning. (The cards give so much intuitive understanding that any attempt to put their total significance in words is to lose their essential message. It is like describing any picture; what is derived from the picture is dependent on the mood and insight of the observer and the depth of his understanding of what he sees.)

Abram is the name of the patriarch of the Jewish people. The literal translation of Abram is 'Mighty Father'. The cryptic significance of Abram is found by laying down, side by side, the four Tarot cards which represent the ideas contained in the four Hebrew letters which spell the name. Anyone who tries this will find that these pictures contain a tremendous amount of information. Within our context here, their message can be stated briefly as 'the initiation of the mighty power within (each of us)'. The word which best expresses the state of consciousness meant by the name Abram is faith.

Later on in the Bible, God changes Abram's name by adding a fifth letter, H, to his name making it Abraham. The literal translation of Abraham is 'Father of a multitude of things (within ourselves)'. The cryptic significance is found by placing the Tarot card for the Hebrew H in the middle of the four cards representing Abram. The additional card changes the meaning of the state of consciousness called Abram. Abraham now means 'the *realization* of the expression of the mighty power within (each of us)'. In short, what was once pure faith is now a faith that we are conscious of and can, therefore, use.

Other cryptic meanings are derived from the numerical correspondences. The following is an example.

In Genesis, 'Abram went in search for Lot (who had been captured by the Edomite kings) and took with him three hundred and eighteen servants born in his own household.' We might ask how Abram, having arrived poor in Canaan, a little over a year before, was able to get to the point of having three hundred and eighteen servants born in his own household. Wherever scripture is translated into nonsense, you can be sure that, there, you will find a message in code.

Abram, as we have suggested, means faith. Lot, decoded, means 'that which is hidden'. So, when in faith you go in search for that which is hidden you are to take three hundred and eighteen servants from your own household (house indicating that which is within). The key to understanding this statement is found in the number 318. Since each Hebrew letter is also a number, we simply substitute the corresponding letters for the number: 300 = *sheen*; 10 = *yod*; 8 = *chayt*; the word that they spell is the verb 'to meditate'. The statement simply means that if you want to find what is hidden, meditate.

In the Book of Revelation, chapter 14, we find, 'A lamb stood on Mt. Zion and with him one hundred and forty four thousand, having his father's name written in their foreheads . . . and they sung a new song and no man could learn that song but the one hundred and forty four thousand which were redeemed from this earth.'

The key to the above statement is in the number 144,000. 100 = *qof*, which means the back of the head; the *medulla oblongata* (in the back of the head) is the source of material, or physical, awareness. 40 = *mem*, which means water or spirit. 4 = *dallet*, indicating the crossing of a threshold. 1,000 means association or advancement. The Biblical phrase then can be read as follows: Those who succeed in advancing their consciousness from the state of material awareness (back of the head) to the forehead (the location of the third eye or *ajna chakra* which, when opened, gives spiritual awareness) are the ones who shall redeem themselves (gain the freedom of their divine nature).

The Qabalistic Level

The Qabalistic level of biblical comprehension is more difficult to describe. This is because it covers a vast amount of information. This level includes all the information held within the symbolism of the Tree of Life with its ten Sephiroth acting in four Qabalistic worlds. It also includes the twenty-two paths which connect the Sephiroth in each of the four worlds and the significance of the over four hundred titles, assignations, and correspondences which are found in the symbolic Qabalah.

Some of the vast amount of symbolism connected with the Symbolic Qabalah is presented graphically in the first chapter.

The Tree of Life, the backbone of the Qabalah, is referred to directly in only two books of the Bible – the first and the last. In the garden of Eden there are two trees. One is the tree of the knowledge of good and evil which God tells Adam (mankind) to leave alone. The other is the tree of life, of which God tells Adam to partake freely.

The name Tree of Life comes from two Hebrew words which can be translated as 'plan or concept of existence'.The diagram of the tree consists of ten Sephiroth or spheres which are arranged in three columns vertically and seven levels horizontally.* The top sphere, called Kether (Crown), represents heaven and the bottom sphere, called Malkuth, represents earth.

Scripture refers often to various aspects of the tree. This is also part of the Qabalistic level of comprehension found in the Bible. In Matthew there are references to the kingdom of heaven. The original Greek word from which heaven is translated is plural. A more accurate translation would be 'kingdom of heavens'. This refers to the seven heavens, or levels, of the Tree of Life.

Solomon's temple with its two columns with a door in between also refers to the tree and its three columns. Christ is crucified between two crosses bearing the two thieves. The two outer columns of the tree represent that which robs us from being 'on the path' or in balance. The center column of the tree is appropriately called the Path.

The Sephira (sphere) on the fourth level on the middle column, half way between heaven and earth is called Tiphareth which means beauty. This is the level of Christ-consciousness. Christ, as with all names in the Bible, refers not to a personage but to a state of consciousness which the man Jesus is said to have achieved. The top sphere, called heaven, is also called 'Father', because heaven refers to 'the heaven within', which cryptically is found in the Hebrew word for father. The Bible

* See pp. 28, 29.

quotes Jesus as saying, 'No one comes to the Father except by me' (John, 14.6). The state of consciousness called Christ which Jesus was personifying is the state of Love. This state on the Tree of Life must be passed through to get from the lowest state to the highest state.

In Matthew (1.17) we find: 'There are fourteen generations from Abraham to David and fourteen generations from David to the carrying away into Babylon and fourteen generations from Babylon to Christ'. The key is the number 14: $10 = yod$ which indicates power; $4 = dallet$ which denotes significant change, or progression. The statement means that there are four major stages of progress: Abraham, the state of consciousness of faith, trust or conviction, which corresponds to the tenth Sephira; David, the state of the recognition of the divine power within, which corresponds to the ninth Sephira; Babylon, a condition of consciousness in which there is confusion, disharmony, or division, which corresponds to the seventh and eighth Sephiroth which are not on the path, signifying the confusion most of us experience in the dichotomy between our thoughts and feelings; Christ, the state of consciousness we call Love, occupies the sixth Sephira on the fourth level of the Tree indicating inner beauty.

Extracting the Creative Principle from Genesis

To discover the Creative Law, Samuel Bousky opened the Bible to the first page. He applied the principles and understanding which he had gained from the Literal and Symbolic Qabalah to the Hebrew.

The source of the Creative Law is the first book of Moses, called Genesis. But Genesis is not the real title of the first book of the Bible. The accepted title comes from the Greek translation of the Hebrew word which means 'generations'. The Hebrew word from which Genesis is derived is not found in the first chapter at all but in the second which reads, 'And these are the generations of the heavens and the earth when they were created'. (Genesis, 2.4.)

Traditionally, the first word of a chapter in Hebrew is also the title. *Breshith* is the first word and therefore the proper title of the chapter. *Breshith* according to Sam means 'the Principle'. The second word in the Hebrew is *bara* which is translated as 'created'. But *bara* can also be translated as 'creates' (present tense). All the English versions imply that we are about to learn how creation was created at some time in the past. It *actually* indicates that we are about to learn the principle of creation *which is active in the present.*

Through mistranslation, the title and meaning of the first chapter was included in the text, thereby hiding its true meaning. Another mistranslation is found in the ending of the first chapter. In the Hebrew, the first three verses of the second chapter are part of the first; all seven days of creation are included in the first chapter.

Placing the first word, *breshith*, in the title, the second word, *bara*, becomes the first word of the first line. The second word is *Elohim* which is translated as 'God' in English. *Elohim* is both a masculine and feminine word, and is plural. To Sam, this word indicates a trinity of divine forces. To me it indicates something else. For the present, we will use Sam's definition of divine forces and discuss them in more detail later.

The phrase which begins the Bible can thus be translated as follows: 'The divine forces create that which to us ('which to us' is normally translated as 'even') is the heavens and that which to us is the earth.'

As we have said, the word 'heavens' refers to the stages of consciousness through which we evolve and these are symbolized in the Tree of Life by the seven levels of the Sephiroth. Earth refers to the material existence symbolized by the tenth Sephira in the lowest of the seven heavens.

This indicates that the *Elohim* are creating not only the physical world but also the emotional, mental and spiritual realms as well.

This is an important point since, in the development of the model of psychometaphysics which we are leading up to, thoughts, feelings, and matter are aspects of one continuous process, and not separate phenomena as commonly assumed.

The next statement in Genesis is a preamble to the seven

days of creation, and not a part of them: 'And the earth was without form and void; and darkness was upon the face of the deep. And the Spirit of God moved upon the face of the waters.' (Genesis, 1.2.)

The words 'without form' are from a Hebrew word which also means superficial; 'upon' is also lofty. 'The face of' is the Hebrew equivalent of awareness. 'Deep' indicates surging waters and Qabalistically refers to the process of visualization. 'Spirit' means breath or that which emanates forward. 'Move' means to hover or concentrate over. 'Waters' denotes visions or imagination.

The preamble to the seven days of creation can thus be translated (or decoded) as follows: 'Our material existence was meaningless and superficial. We are unaware of the potential we would have in an elevated awareness so the essence of the divine forces within us (our spiritual selves) are concentrating on this awareness to attain the heights of creativity.' Another way of reading this is: 'The divine forces within us vitalize an imaginative activity through the concentration of awareness.'

The First Day of Creation

'And God said, Let there be light: And there was light. And God saw the light, that it was good: and God divided the light from the darkness. And God called the light Day and the darkness he called Night. And the evening and the morning were the first day.' (Genesis, 1.3-5.)*

'Said' means desire or determination. 'Light' is illumination or comprehension. 'Day' is the present or awareness of the now, and refers to a stage in a process. 'Night' means obscure or unawareness of the present. In the first day there are four basic qualities referred to, which we can place under the heading of determination: desire (from the word 'said'), awareness (in the sense of changing from an unaware state to an aware state), decision (determination to effect a change), and selection (the identification of what is to be changed).

It is interesting to note that at the end of each 'day' the Bible

* This description of the first day and those following are paraphrases of the biblical text used by Samuel Bousky.

says: 'And the evening and the morning were the . . . day.' As we grow in awareness, at first we don't comprehend (evening) and then we do (morning). In modern thinking, we would, of course, refer to a day as morning and night. 'Day' refers to a stage in a process and not a definite period of time.

The Second Day

'And God said, Let there be a firmament in the midst of the waters, and let it divide the waters from the waters.' To paraphrase the text, the waters below the firmament were divided from those above.

'Firmament' is from the verb to pound or make firm. It means to make firm a distinction. 'Waters' denotes imaginative thoughts or the process of visualization. On the second day, then, a distinction is made between a visualization which we intend to materialize and one which we do not. The second day describes an evaluation which follows the determination of the first day (stage).

The Third Day

On the third day the water is gathered together to let dry land appear. The land is called earth and the land brings forth grass, herbs, and fruit trees yielding seed after its own kind. This stage which talks about the bringing forth of life for the first time we will refer to as the stage of conception.

The Fourth Day

'And God said, Let there be lights in the firmament of the heaven to divide the day from the night; and let them be for signs, and for seasons, and for days, and years: . . . and God made two great lights . . . to rule the day and the night . . . he made the stars also . . . And the evening and the morning were the fourth day.' (Genesis, 1.14-19.)

The sun, moon, and stars, etc. form the background of the manifestation to come. We will refer to this stage of our creative process as attitude, since it is the mental framework or background for our individual creative endeavor.

The Fifth Day

'And God said, Let the waters bring forth abundantly the moving creature that hath life, and fowl that may fly above the earth . . . God created great whales, and every living creature' that moves in the waters. (Genesis, 1.20-23.)

This stage has to do with movement above and below the waters (the visualization) and refers to the feeling or emotion we add to our process of visualization.

The Sixth Day

On the sixth day God creates the living creatures of the earth – cattle, beasts, creeping things, etc. He creates Man in his own image, both male and female and gives Man, 'dominion over the earth and all that is upon it.' (Genesis, 1.24-31.)

The key to the sixth stage is that God creates a duplication or reflection of himself, Man, in the visualization process.

The Seventh Day

'On the seventh day God ended his work which he had made; and he rested on the seventh day from all his work which he had made. And God blessed the seventh day, and sanctified it: because that in it he had rested from all his work which God created and made.' (Genesis, 2.2-3.)

This statement, in bad English, is actually a mistranslation. It more correctly should read: 'And God blessed the seventh day and sanctified it because in it rested all the work which God created *to be made.*' The two statements indicate two different stages of creation. First the creative act takes place in the spiritual realm, then the formation occurs in the physical. The Samuel Bousky translation states that the creative act has already taken place in the spiritual realm, but the formation has not yet occurred. This stage of the creative process is a stage of expectant inactivity or gestation.

The seven days of creation, then, describe a process which occurs within each of us.

Since the process is indicated as occurring on the 'spiritual plane' it is something that we do within ourselves. This is a meditation done without any outward physical activity. 'Spiritual' is simply an archaic way of referring to the essential self or the 'I' of the individual.

The model of psychometaphysics, which we are leading up to, is an attempt to describe the nature of the 'I'. At this point in our search, suffice it to say that in using the Creative Law you will experience, more directly than words can indicate, the basic, creative nature of your 'I'.

The Bible says that Man is created in the image and likeness of God. The Hebrew word for image comes from the verb 'to shade'. The noun means shadow, fantasy, illusion, or resemblance. The noun, translated as 'likeness', means resemblance, similitude, model, or likeness in the sense of a blood relationship. The word image suggests that we are not talking about the body, personality, character structure, or ego of man but some non-physical aspect. The phrase means that Man is the duplication of a divine essence (called God). In the New Testament Jesus states that it is not he (his physical personage) who does the work but that it is the father within who does it.

You are not your body, mind, or personality. These are the activities of the real 'you' which is a spiritual essence. This spiritual essence is like God. It is basically creative.

The Principles of the Creative Law

The Creative Law is actuated by using two basic creative capabilities: creative imagination and feeling. It also requires faith in its deepest sense.

We tend to think of faith as mental or intellectual acceptance. The word in Hebrew is translated as faith, belief, or conviction. In the biblical Book of Hebrews it says, 'Faith is the substance of things hoped for, the evidence of things unseen.' Faith is the basis of things expected or the evidence of things yet to be experienced. Also in Hebrews, we find, 'Through faith we understand that the worlds were framed by the word of God so that things which are seen are not made of things which do appear.' God, under the name Jehovah, means the power of the divine essence within us. In Hebrew, 'word' means exhalation or expression. Samuel Bousky decodes this to mean, 'Your worlds (things you are involved in) are created by the expression of the divine capability within you.' Faith, then, is a motivating pattern within your inner consciousness. It is the investment you have made in your deepest expectations about yourself and life. Faith is manifested in your actions and feeling and not necessarily by your words and thoughts.

There are three basic principles of creativity: first, a union must occur between the male and female aspects of our nature; second, there has to be a vitalization; third, there must be some direction which guides the process to fruition.

The male aspect can be called determination. The female aspect is visualization. The union occurs through the channel of activated intelligence or imagination. The switch which turns the process on (vitalization) is feeling or emotion.

The key to all dynamic processes, including the Creative Law, is the Tetragrammaton in the Qabalah. The Tetragrammaton is the 'Name', translated as 'Lord' in the Authorized Version, and as 'Jehovah' in the Revised Version, of the Bible. The Tetragrammaton is not the name of a personage. It is a cryptic formula related to the Hebrew verb 'to be'. Its closest translation is: 'That which was, that which is, and that which will be.' This 'Name' is spelled *yod-hay-vav-hay*. It is the fourfold process called God, as described in Chapter One.

Any dynamic system has the four aspects of force, pattern, activity and form (which the Tetragrammaton refers to). To sprinkle a lawn you need the force of the water pressure, the pattern (structure) of the hose to guide the force, the activity of the water moving through the hose, and the form or result which is the watering of the lawn.

These four aspects echo throughout the Bible in both its construction and what it says. In Revelation there are the four beasts: the lion, eagle, bull, and man. (Aside from their biblical significance, they represent the four fixed signs of the zodiac.) The four gospels of Mark, Matthew, Luke, and John portray Christ as a servant, king, man, and divine being.

The Creative Law has these four aspects within it. Determination is the force, visualization is the patterning, emotion is the activating factor, and the fourth aspect, form, corresponds to the gestation period in which the process is allowed to bring forth its result.

These four principles can be applied to the physical world as a whole. The forces of the physical world are the gravitational, electromagnetic, and the strong and weak nuclear forces. Samuel Bousky equates the pattern or structural aspect with space itself. The activity is time. The form is matter.

There is an old Qabalistic doctrine which states: 'As it is above, so it is below.' Sam has taken this to indicate that there are spiritual equivalents to these four physical manifestations of force, pattern, activity, and form. According to him the analogous spiritual dimension corresponding to physical space is existence. Corresponding to the dimension of time is consciousness (awareness of existence). The fourth aspect, relating to matter, he refers to as something akin to the Sanskrit *akasha*. The only word in English which may be adequate is 'etheric' (matter). In the spiritual world, there is something which has the qualities of matter, which acts as a recording medium. The *akasha*, or etheric matter, records all events in consciousness as our bodies record all the events in our lives.

Corresponding to the forces of physics are the forces of the spiritual realm. Sam's conception of the spiritual forces is based on the name Elohim. The name of God in Genesis who creates the world is Elohim. God, known by this name, is 'The only one God from which all things come.' The name is both masculine and feminine and is plural. The first syllable, *El* is composed of *aleph lammed*. *Aleph* indicates divine energy; *lammed* indicates that which stimulates. The *El*, then, indicates the idea of force. Since Elohim is plural, then it must indicate forces.

The only words in the Bible, also translated as God, which are compounds containing the syllable *El* are: El Chaddai which decodes as 'life'; El Elom which decodes as 'mind'; and El Elyon which means 'soul'. Sam considers the three forces of the spiritual world, collectively known under the name Elohim, to be the life force, mind force, and soul force.

Further, he considers that the three forces which operate in the spiritual world affect us in different ways. The life force sustains life as we know it. The mind force causes our thoughts and self-consciousness. The soul force stimulates our personal growth. Sam believes also that it is these three forces which are referred to as the 'Father, Son, and Holy Ghost'.

This decoding of the name Elohim to indicate the forces of life, mind and soul implies a certain kind of cosmogony. In this picture of reality, the self seems to be subject to these pre-existing forces whose source remains unknown. If it is true that the life force sustains all life-forms including ourselves and the soul force stimulates our evolutionary growth in conscious-ness and the mind force produces our self-consciousness and the very thoughts that we think, then what is left for the self to do? Is it the self that initiates the creative process? Or does the mind force produce the creative thought at the urging of the soul force? What then is the self?

In part two, entitled 'Psychometaphysics', I will derive a radically different interpretation of the name Elohim, and therefore a different cosmogony. Although Sam and I differ on this point, our differences have no effect on the efficacy of the Creative Law.

The fact is that the Creative Law works. I have used it, as have many of my students and friends. I have found it in many forms, for example in Maxwell Maltz' *Psychocybernetics*.[13] Sev-eral growth-oriented psychotherapies and training courses use it. And elements of the creative process are used in Gestalt Therapy and Psychosynthesis, as well as being incorporated in self-improvement schemes including hypnosis techniques.

As with any real law of nature, it works whether or not you are conscious of it or believe in it. Everyone uses it and is affected by it even though it remains deeply unconscious for the over-whelming majority of people on this planet.

The Technique of the Creative Law

Introduction

I hope that in presenting the Creative Law technique in its practical form that the reader may recognize it as a process he or she is already using to some degree. I also believe that it is much better to learn the technique first hand from someone who knows how to use it, and is aware of the effects it can have on one's life, rather than to attempt to get it from a book.

I am presenting it here because it exemplifies the process described later under the heading 'The Co-Creation' in the second part of this work. To describe these creative processes philosophically would, I believe, tend to give the reader the idea that the processes are spoken of in a metaphorical way. Neither the Creative Law nor the process of the Co-Creation of Matter and Consciousness are metaphors or parables. They are the practical means whereby creation takes place on both personal and universal levels.

The First Stage

The first stage is concerned with your determination. There are four aspects of determination which should be considered: 1) you must be aware of or believe that there is something available to you which will better your life in some way; 2) you must have a real desire to get what you want; 3) you must make a firm decision to do something about obtaining what you want; 4) you must select precisely what it is that you want as an end result.

The Second Stage

The second stage is one of consolidation. In this stage you must evaluate the desire which motivates you to want what you have chosen in the first stage. Is what you desire now what you will want later? Are you sure what you want the end result to be? Is it the ultimate goal or something only part way toward gaining it? Through this stage of evaluation you must make firm your selection of the end result.

Check with yourself and see if it is really all right if: 1) you use this technique for getting what you want (some with conventional religious upbringing may find this a difficult question); 2) it is correct, in your own estimation, to get what you want. If the answer to either of these questions is 'no' then simply do not use this process until you feel right about doing it.

The Third Stage

The third stage is the conception stage. You must conceive a visionary activity (use your imagination) that indicates or intimates that what you want *has already taken place*. Your mental scene must show that what you desire is already yours. You must contrive a scene which you can easily believe. You must see yourself as a participant in your scene.

The Fourth Stage

The fourth stage is concerned with your background attitude. Your attitude produces the motivating feeling with which you will vitalize your creative process. Your attitude is carried forward through the process and will effect the result.

If your attitude toward what you are doing is negative then the result of your effort may well turn out to be destructive for you, rather than creative. There is no morality built into it. It is simply that you will 'reap what you sow'. By 'negative', I mean an attitude of doing it out of fear, anxiety, disgust, revenge, or with the intent to do harm or manipulate someone. By positive attitude I mean doing it out of charity, empathy, gratitude, or joy. This means that a positive state of mind is required. To try to undo something with your creative power is less effective than creating something better in its place.

Secondly, don't be a 'do-gooder'. Your attitude may not be as pure as you think it is. *Don't interfere with other people's lives.* If you are trying to impress someone then you're missing the point. This process is for you to become more in touch with your deepest nature, not to enhance your ego.

The Fifth Stage

Stages one to four are really planning stages. The fifth stage is where you actually begin to do something. Sit back and close your eyes. Get a feeling of being centered deep within yourself. Allow yourself to relax as fully as you can while remaining totally awake. Play through the scene you have been planning in your imagination. It is very important that you see yourself as participating in the scene as an actor plays a role. Do not see yourself outside the scene as if you were watching a movie or you will not be a participant in the result. Run through the scene in the *present tense*. In your imagination you should be participating in a scene that is happening now. If you set it up to happen in the future or past it will *always* be happening in the future or past and you will never experience it in reality.

While running through your scene, do it with deep feeling. Experience now the feeling you would have if the scene desired was *actually taking place*. Feeling is what turns the switch on and makes it happen. The emotion you add to your scene is what vitalizes it. The more fervently you can create the appropriate feeling, the better.

It is also important to bring your senses into play. See yourself and the scene in as much detail as you can. Touch, taste, smell, and hear as much of what you are creating as you can. Some people have difficulty visualising the scene in pictures. Don't let this stop you. It is the intent and basic ideas which are important and not a three-dimentional color vision; remember that, in imagination, what you place there is simply there because you intend it to be there. It will remain as long as your intent remains.

The Sixth Stage

The sixth stage has to do with reflection and conviction. The scene you have created with its emotional content is a reflection of your desire. In another sense, the scene is reflected back to you. Although it often does not occur in the first few times you try this technique, you will feel something happen within you as you energize the scene with your emotion. You will gain a feeling of conviction, a sense that the scene is taking hold. It is feed-back from your emotional circuitry.

The Seventh Stage

The seventh step requires that you stop your effort and 'rest expectantly'. Here, you take your mind off what you have done and allow the universe to bring it forth into manifestation. This is the gestation process. After planting your seed do not disturb it.

To nourish your creation simply know that it is on the way to fruition. The Bible indicates that harvest time *always* follows seed time.

Here are some additional helpful hints that you may find valuable in using the Creative Law:

1. Many people find it difficult to pick out something which they really want in life. It is best to find something simple to try at first, to prove that you can do it successfully. When Samuel Bousky first taught it to me he suggested using the creative process to find a quarter (American 25 cent piece). Out of twenty-two people present who tried this eighteen were successful in the period of one week. Another 'test' is to use it to find a parking space in front of or near some place you are going to in the city in the near future. Another simple exercise is to have some long-lost friend contact you again through writing or calling you on the phone. The confidence you gain from starting with these simple things will help you when you are attempting something much more important.

Among other things you may want to do with the process is changing bad habits. For example, if you examine the way you worry about things that may happen in the future, you may notice that you are using the same process to create for yourself something you don't want. Rather than worrying about getting a job, or passing an examination, set up your scene showing yourself as having got the job or having passed the exam.

The creative process can be used to improve many aspects of your life. You can improve your memory, state of being, thinking habits, your health, and change the circumstances of your life in many ways.

2. Make your scene as general as possible at first. If you are inexperienced in using the process and you have not yet established a firm belief in its effectiveness, do not try for miracles. Your imaginative scene should not include such details as time factors and specific ways in which you want your results to take place. So in finding a coin, for example, do not visualize the exact time and place in which you will find it. Your scene should generally imply a place and you should leave the time it takes you to find it to 'circumstance'.

An effective way of being general and dealing with difficult scenes is to set up a scene showing you and a friend having a conversation. In the imaginary conversation hear yourself saying to your friend that you have received or achieved what you wanted.

3. It is fine to repeat the creative process to get something. Allow time to pass before you repeat it for the same thing. Once or twice a day is sufficient. Used too often it loses its effectiveness. When repeating it, always have the attitude that it is already on its way to fruition and that you are helping it along.

4. Remember that it will take time for your creative efforts to manifest in your experience. Be patient. You have been doing this process unconsciously for years. It may take some time for your old unconscious creations to be replaced by your conscious ones.

5. The seven stages of the creative process are actually one stage. If you were perfectly clear about what you wanted, and had no conflicting mental attitudes or doubtful feelings, then what you received would be a perfect reflection of your intent. After practising the seven stages for a while, you may find that you only need to intend for your intention to become manifest.

Additional References in the Bible

Other statements can be found in scripture which refer to the Creative Law: Jesus said, 'When you pray, enter into your closet and, when you have shut the door, pray to your father which is in secret and your father which seeth in secret will reward you openly.' (Matthew, 6.6)

Jesus said, 'When you pray, believe that you have already received and you shall have it.' (Some Bibles mistranslate this as 'will receive'.) (Mark, 11.24) And, 'Commit thy works unto the Lord (inner power of being) and thy thoughts shall be established.' (Proverbs, 16.3)

The fourth commandment reads: 'Observe the sabbath day to keep it holy as Jehovah, your God, commanded you. Six days shall you labor and do all your work, but the seventh is a sabbath to Jehovah, your God. In it you shall not do any work, not you or your son or your daughter or your man-servant or your maid-servant or your ox or your ass or any of your cattle or the sojourner within your gates that your man-servant and maid-servant may rest as well as you.'

'Jehovah, your God' means the creative power of being within you; 'son' means the act of using your creative capability; 'daughter' is your ability to conceptualize; 'man-servant' means anxiety; 'maid-servant' means fear; 'ox', in this case, means your ability to analyse; 'ass' refers to a reassessment; 'cattle' means inner turmoil; 'sojourner' is alienation; 'gate' indicates thought.

To paraphrase the fourth commandment according to Samuel Bousky: 'Remember, in the release stage, to maintain it faithfully as your inner divinity requires. Maintain your activity through six stages, but the seventh stage is a release to your inner divinity. During it, there shall be no activity, not within you, nor of your creative power, nor of your conceptive ability. Do not be anxious, fearful. Do not analyse or reassess it. Do not allow any alienation or turmoil to fill your thoughts, so that your anxiety and fear may rest as well as you.'

Postscript

What all this implies is that each of us is experiencing now exactly what we have created for ourselves. All human beings on this planet live in a pure democracy (all political connotations aside). Each of our innermost desires counts as one vote in the overall election of reality.

At first, this suggestion seems highly unlikely. Even if we ourselves are not suffering in some way, we know of many whose circumstances leave much to be desired. Why, then, are people creating misery for themselves? Why is mankind often imposing war, starvation, slavery, and repression on itself?

Could it be that the Creative Law operates in a destructive way when left unconscious? Perhaps those who are consciously using their creative capabilities are more successful in life than those who are not or don't know about it.

Perhaps those who believe that fate or some outside God is the only source of their circumstance find themselves unmotivated to seek their own personal creative capacity. Perhaps it is a religion, philosophy, or political system which reinforces and sustains the idea that circumstance cannot be overcome by the individual. Do we not tend to believe that some God, or leader, or society itself, is ultimately responsible?

Perhaps it is because most people do not have direct experience of their own true nature as creative beings. Most of us are still identified with being a body or a mind and can conceive of nothing more. Perhaps we are at the stage of evolution in which survival is still the motivating factor in most of our lives and these so-called spiritual endeavors are left to those who are already surviving successfully. Perhaps all of these factors contribute to the way things are.

The purpose of this work is to help change all that. It is my belief that once people get in touch with their true natures and utilize their creative capabilities *consciously* the world will be a much better place. I base this belief on the assumption that each of us essentially wants the same thing: a harmonious life of fulfilling work and loving relationships with others, based on the freedom and dignity of the individual. I believe that if consciousness is increased by each individual then social systems will evolve which will reflect and aid the evolution of consciousness for all.

I realize that this is a Utopian vision and that Utopias are frowned upon these days. But if you had your choice, isn't that what you would want? But my purpose in writing this is not to describe a Utopia. It is to describe the nature of reality as it is now. From this description certain things will be seen as keys to improving life as we know it. The model of Psychometaphysics which follows, and the subsequent chapter on a method of consciousness expansion called Enlightenment Intensive hold some important and practical keys to bringing about this improvement.

PART TWO
PSYCHOMETAPHYSICS

4
The Model of Psychometaphysics

Introduction

Psychometaphysics is based on many things – the philosophy and techniques of the various schools of Humanistic Psychology, the teachings of Charles Berner* and Samuel Bousky, and the philosophy and methods of Qabalah.

The model of Psychometaphysics is presented with reference to the Qabalah because it lends itself so well to the organization of the information that I want to present. My intent in doing so is to show how this most ancient of metaphysical systems may have been pointing at similar truths and conclusions. Psychometaphysics, however, is not an attempt to replace the Qabalah. The Qabalah is not only a philosophy but also a method of gaining truth, as well as organizing information. Psychometaphysics is simply one interpretation of Qabalah.

In great part the model of Psychometaphysics is based on the experience and teachings of Charles Berner, the originator of the Enlightenment Intensive. I have, however, not presented anything in the model of Psychometaphysics which I have taken as fact without testing it 'in the laboratory' of my own experience.

Psychometaphysics, as I have said, is my answer to the question 'What is Life?' It is a mental construct built within the limitations of words and diagrams. As with all written philosophies, it is not the truth itself but a way of pointing at the truth with symbols. It is my 'head trip' about the nature of the universe. It is incomplete and must always remain so. No amount of words and symbols can capture life itself. Life will always remain the most wonderful and amazing mystery no matter how accurately we may think we have pinned it down.

* He has since changed his name to Yogeshwar Muni.

Alternative Overviews of the Four Worlds

We begin our description of the universe with a look at the whole of it as symbolized by the Qabalistic model. The following few pages are graphic representations of the whole of life (in its broadest sense of everything existing) or Positive Existence. I present them here to show the various ways you can see the four worlds of the Qabalah. In the discussions that follow we will jump from one of these overviews to another as we seek the meaning behind their symbolism.

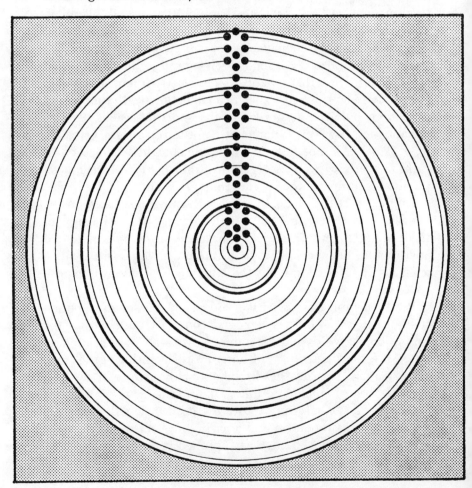

The overview opposite shows the four worlds arranged in concentric circles. Negative Existence (the dotted area) surrounds the four worlds and contains them. The largest circle contains the Tree of Life of the world of Atziluth. Atziluth contains Briah which contains Yetzirah, all of which contain the last of the four worlds Assiah. The order of the generation of the worlds moves from Negative Existence, surrounding the circles, into the center.

Another possible overview, on the next page, shows the four worlds as overlapping one another.

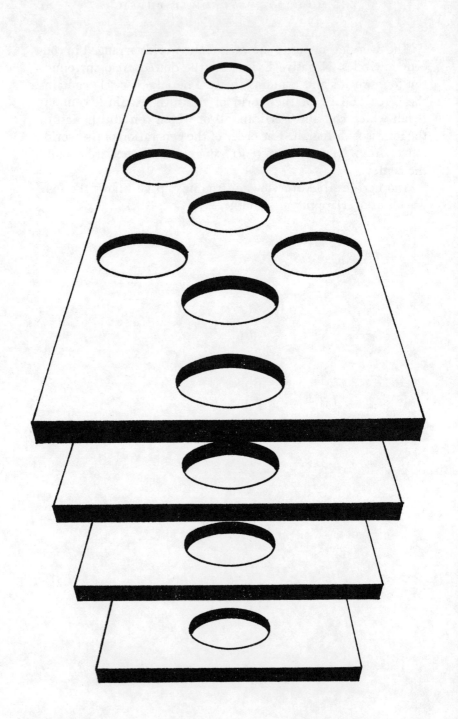

The Meaning of the Four Worlds

The key to understanding the functions of each of the four Qabalistic worlds is found in the Tetragrammaton. It denotes the four-fold process conveying aspects of Force (*yod*), Pattern (*hay*), Activity (*vav*), and Form (*hay*). On the macrocosmic scale, each of the four worlds corresponds functionally to one of these qualities.

The four Trees of Life which follow are drawn and labelled as they are found in the Qabalistic literature available today. They are presented here to illustrate the transition from the classical Qabalistic model to the model of Psychometaphysics.

EHEIEH

JEHOVAH
ELOHIM

JEHOVAH

ELOHIM
GEBOR

EL

ELOAH
VADAATH

ELOHIM
TZABOATH

JEHOVAH
TZABOATH

SHADDAI
EL CHAI

ADONAI
MELEKH

ATZILUTH

Atziluth: The World of Ability

The first world to be created out of Negative Existence is called Atziluth, 'The Boundless World of Divine Names'. This is the highest spiritual world of Qabalah. Each of the ten names of the Creator assigned to this world indicate a different aspect of the essential Self of what is translated in English as 'God'.

With respect to the Tetragrammaton, Atziluth corresponds to the first letter, *yod*. *Yod* indicates the idea of force. Force, in a personal sense, is the same as ability. Force is measured as the ability to do something or interact with something. Therefore the Sephiroth of the World of Atziluth indicate the ten basic abilities that the Creator has.

The first Sephira then indicates the ability that the Creator has 'to be' (Eheieh means 'I shall be'). The second Sephira, containing the name Jehovah, indicates the ability of the Creator 'to do'. The other eight Sephiroth should, then, indicate eight other abilities which the Creator has.

In the model of Psychometaphysics, the World of Atziluth is changed to 'The World of Ability'.

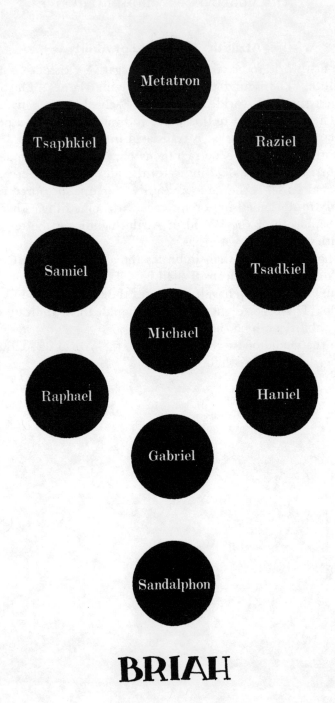

BRIAH

Briah: The World of Mind

The second Qabalistic world to emerge out of Negative Existence following the sequence of the first world is Briah, 'The Archangelic World of Creations'. Briah corresponds to the second letter of the Tetragrammaton, *hay*, which indicates the quality of pattern. Briah represents the patterning or organization of the abilities or forces named in the first world of Atziluth.

Traditionally, archangels are the highest ranking messengers of God. They are the foremen who oversee and direct the work that God has intended. They also represent God to all 'lower' beings. It is written that no one (i.e. human being) can contact or see God directly but must communicate with Him through His representatives, in this case His archangels.

Analogous to the archangels of God is the mind in Man. It is the ideas, concepts, viewpoints, and images of the mind which act as patterning functions with respect to the essential Self, or Quantum God, in humans. It is the mind which forms and patterns the primary intentionality of a Quantum God into specific activities of the personality. It is the mind which patterns the character structure through which the Quantum God relates to the world and others. It is only through this pattern that Quantum Gods contact and communicate with each other.

In the model of Psychometaphysics, Briah becomes the World of Mind. Each of the Sephiroth on the Tree of Life in this world are seen as indicating some aspect of mentality or character structure.

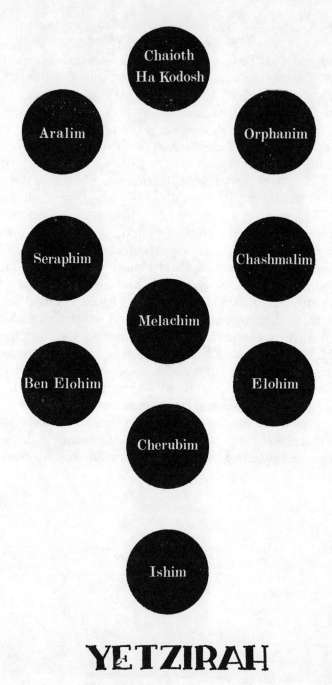

YETZIRAH

Yetzirah: The World of Body

From the second world of Briah emerges Yetzirah, 'The Hierarchal World of Formation'. Yetzirah corresponds to the third letter of the Tetragrammaton, *vav*, which indicates the quality of activity. The abilities of the first world are patterned in the second world and become active in this, the third world.

The Sephiroth of Yetzirah are named after powers, energies, and angels. Angels are God's workers who are under the directorship of the archangels (mind). Analogous to the angels and powers of God in the Qabalah are the sensations, feelings and emotions of a human being. These are the result of energy transactions within the body as it functions in the world.

The tenth Sephira in Yetzirah is called Ishim, 'The souls of Just Men'. The soul of a human being is associated with his feeling nature. The soul is seen as a body but one which survives and is antecedent to the physical body. Since Yetzirah emerges from the World of Mind (patterning) and is within it, it is not referring to the structure of the body which is its form but to its activity or functional aspect. The body, seen functionally, is a structure which allows for a wide range of energy functions. It can be seen as the organized activity of a multitude of life processes. The body is also a unique expression of a Quantum God who is expressing his inner nature through his physical functioning.

In the model of Psychometaphysics, Yetzirah becomes the World of the Body, the energy functions of the Quantum God as they are patterned by his mental constitution. The World of Body is concerned with the processes and activities of energy in and around the physical body.

Rashith Ha Gilgalim

Primum Mobile

Shabbathai

Saturn

Masloth

Zodiac

Madim

Mars

Tzedeg

Jupiter

Shemesh

the Sun

Kokab

Mercury

Nogah

Venus

Levanah

the Moon

Cholom Yosodoth

the four elements

ASSIAH

Assiah: The World of Matter

Fourth in the sequence of emerging worlds is Assiah, 'The Elemental World of Substances'. Assiah corresponds to the fourth letter of the Tetragrammaton, *heh*, which indicates the idea of pattern carried forth into manifestation as form or substance. The ability or force of the first world is patterned in the World of Mind, activated in the World of Body, and formalized materially in this, the fourth world.

But the Qabalah reminds us that all the worlds are contained in Negative Existence and that there is no real time sequence. The first Sephira in the first world is in the tenth Sephira of the fourth world and vice versa. We have been describing the worlds as having emerged out of Negative Existence in a sequence suggested by our description of them. We might be more accurate to see them as simultaneous expressions of a Quantum God.

The first Sephira in Assiah is designated as 'The Primum Mobile', or 'First Swirlings'. It might ideally be symbolized as a center point or dot representing a source or beginning. This is the same symbol that I have chosen to represent the Creator Himself in the chapter entitled 'The Path of the Dot' at the beginning of this book. The correlation suggests to me that matter and consciousness are simultaneous creations.

The tenth Sephira in Assiah is called 'The Sphere of the Four Elements'. The four elements, of course, refer to the four aspects of the Tetragrammaton – Force, Pattern, Activity, and Form. This, the last Sephira of the Qabalistic creation, represents the whole of creation functioning in the realm of substance. Matter is the result of all the Sephiroth of all the four worlds functioning as one process simultaneously.

In the model of Psychometaphysics, Assiah becomes the World of Matter. It is in the World of Matter that we begin to describe the emerging model of reality.

5
The World of Matter

The Microcosmic World of Matter

Our description of matter begins in the tenth sphere of the fourth world.

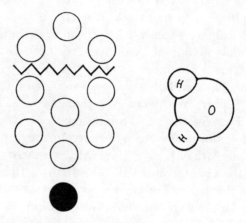

The Tenth Sephira: The Molecule

A molecule is the smallest physical unit of matter which retains the property of its substance. The smallest unit of water which has the qualities of water is one molecule of water. If we divide it further it ceases to be water and becomes one atom of oxygen attached to two atoms of hydrogen both of which have properties entirely different from water.

All physical things are composed of molecules. They are responsible for all mechanical, chemical, and biological phenomena. The rate at which they oscillate creates the effects we call temperature and pressure and determines whether a substance is in a liquid, gaseous, or solid state.

Molecules are the smallest units of matter which interact with the five senses. The whole bodily experience of the physical world comes into awareness through the seeing, hearing, touching, tasting, and smelling of matter on a molecular scale. Sense perception arises when the highly organized molecules of the body interact with molecules in the environment.

Molecules are so small that we do not usually see them individually but only in huge conglomerates (some forms of plastic can be considered to be one large molecule, big enough to hold in your hand). The size of molecules range below one millionth of a centimeter. There are millions of different molecules ranging from the relatively simple water molecule to the complex megamolecules of biology.

Moving up the tree, we see matter on an even smaller scale.

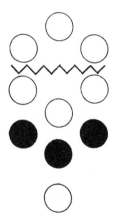

The Seventh, Eighth and Ninth Sephiroth: The Atom

All molecules are composed of the elements. The smallest unit of an element which retains the properties of that element is an atom. An atom can be as small as one hundred thousandth of the size of the molecule. A hundred million atoms can fit into a cubic centimeter.

We are reducing matter to its primary structural components as we re-focus our hypothetical microscope. The physical universe is composed of tens of millions of compounds which are in turn composed of millions of kinds of molecules which are composed of just over one hundred kinds of atoms (the elements)

which, in turn, are composed of three things. Atoms are composed of electrons, protons, and neutrons. But the overwhelm-
ingly major component of an atom is space.

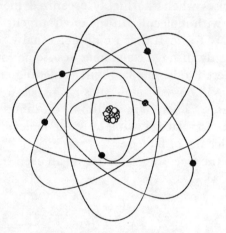

To get an idea of the structure of an atom, imagine yourself
outside a large football stadium. Electrons the size of marbles
are passing overhead in their orbit so that you are standing on
what would be the outer edge of the sphere of the atom. The
nucleus of the atom is in the center of the football field. The
neutrons and protons which compose the nucleus, and contain
most of its mass, would also be the size of marbles. From this
vantage point you can see that the atom, the building block of
all matter is mostly space. The volume of an atom is determined
by the outer shell of orbiting electrons. Over ninety per cent of
the mass (weight) of the atom is in the nucleus, which takes up
little more than a millionth of the volume of the whole atom.

The only difference between an atom of one element and an
atom of another is the number of neutrons, protons, and electrons it has. The electron field determines the properties of the
element and how it reacts with other elements. The nucleus does
not appear to take part in chemical reactions.

On the level of the atom we have long passed the scale of
things which we call material.

The picture of an atom as a 'thing' composed of small bil-
liard ball-like particles in orbits is obsolete. The atom is now

seen as a field containing polar singularities which have a tendency to be located in certain parts of the field in a highly
random fashion, indeterminate except in terms of probability.
The field, which is the whole of the atom, is densest in the locale
of the atom as we think of its extent, but each atom can be said
to occupy the whole of the universe. Each atom in the universe
exerts a force on every other atom in the universe but since the
force of influence is dependent on the distance between one atom
and another, atoms which are far apart appear to have no influence on each other with respect to our ability to measure it.
Large accumulations of atoms such as planets and stars, as we
know, have a great gravitational influence over vast distances.

The molecular level of matter has been assigned to the tenth
Sephira. The electron, proton, and neutron which make up the
atom have been assigned to the seventh, eighth and ninth Sephiroth. Now we move into the scale of the nucleus, less than 10^{-12}
cm. in size.

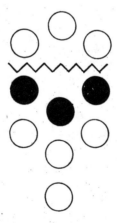

The Fourth, Fifth and Sixth Sephiroth: Sub-atomic Particles

Atomic nuclei are composed of even smaller particles called
sub-atomic particles. These 'particles' have no resemblence to
matter as we sense and think of it at all. The technology needed
to deal with them is so advanced that it jumps from physics to
nuclear physics, including quantum mechanics and relativity
which are basically mathematics.

These particles are created by a particle accelerator which

produces collisions between nuclear material in a bubble chamber. In a bubble chamber there is a charged molecular medium in which tracks are left by particles passing through. The tracks are photographed at high speed (some of the particles last for only billionths of a second). The nature of the particles is classified according to the direction, curvature, and length of its path. Over four hundred sub-atomic particles have been named so far. The properties of the particles are converted into mathematical language and are fed into computers. The data is then placed in the hands of the theoretical physicists who are trying to derive a theory or model which will describe the nature and behavior of these, the smallest components of matter known to man.

Professor Murry Gell-Mann and his associates suggest that it is possible, although it remains a hypothesis at the time of this writing, that all sub-atomic particles are the result of the activity of three even more primary particles. They have been called quarks. Quarks in fact may not exist as small particles, but might be just mathematical abstractions.

If Gell-Mann is correct, then quarks act together in such a way as to give the appearance of sub-atomic particles which, in turn, act together to yield the neutrons, protons, and electrons which act to produce the appearance of atoms which combine to form molecules, megamolecules, cells, tissues, organs, and bodies. The bodies, thus constituted, are in turn, busy looking into bubble chambers. So what is looking at what?

If in fact quarks exist we can no longer call them physical. On the scale of quarks we are not looking at matter but merely our thoughts about matter. There is nothing substantial about a quark. It is a thought about matter and is therefore purely psychological in nature. In order to delve deeper into the nature of matter we will have to understand the nature of thought.

At this point objectivity folds back on itself. The boundary of subject and object becomes blurred. What is happening is that one form of matter is busy analyzing another form of matter as if they were unconnected. The only difference is the scale of the viewpoint from which they are looking.

Pierre Teilhard de Chardin in *The Phenomenon of Man*[14]

writes: 'The time has come to realize that an interpretation of
the universe, even a positivist one, remains unsatisfying unless
it covers the interior as well as the exterior of things; mind as
well as matter. The true physics is that which will, one day,
achieve the inclusion of Man in his wholeness in a coherent
picture of the world.'

It is at this point that we come to the Abyss of the World of
Matter. To paraphrase astronomer James Jeans, the universe
looks less and less like a machine and more and more like a great
thought. The dividing line between mechanism and thought in
the Tree of Life is the Abyss.

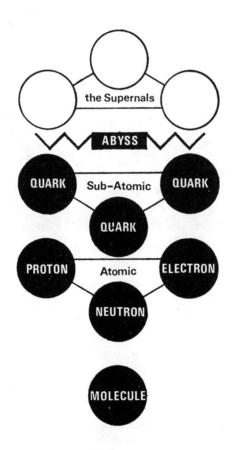

The microcosmic World of Matter up to the Abyss

The Macrocosmic World of Matter

Spiral in Ursa Major from the Hale Observatories

The universe, as science sees it at present, consists of an indef-inite number of island galaxies, all of which appear to be moving away from each other at tremendous speeds. One hypoth-esis states that these galaxies are the remnants of a primordial explosion called the 'Big Bang' which filled the universe with matter. The matter then coalesced into galaxies, solar systems, and planets. There is an additional hypothesis which states that there was no definitive beginning of the universe but that it periodically contracts and explodes and has always done so.

Recent estimates of the mass of the universe suggest, however, that there is not enough mass to reverse the present trend of expansion, according to the known laws of physics. This suggests that the universe is in a steady state of creation as proposed by Bondi, Gold, and Hoyle in their 'continuous creation' theory. Although this hypothesis violates the assumption that matter cannot be created or destroyed, the assumption may be a result of our limited viewpoint. For instance, Einstein's relativity has been demonstrated as accurate for phenomena occurring at high speeds and long distances but it is not obvious to someone viewing phenomena locally at slow speeds and short distances. Perhaps the conservation of energy and mass laws we accept in our laboratories do not apply to outer space. Whatever our hypothesis is concerning the origin of the universe, it apparently has emerged out of a nothingness or is continuing to do so. Scientists are reluctant to hypothesize this apparent creation of something out of nothing, simply because it transcends the bounds of current scientific thought.

Unlike the universe as a whole, our galaxy, the Milky Way, does have a center. Scientists looking into the center of the galaxy see the remnants of the hypothetical explosion which formed the galaxy. Surrounding the center they see rings of hot ionized gas and tremendous amounts of electromagnetic radiation. These rings appear to be the remnants of a primal 'explosion' of the same order as the 'Big Bang' which formed the universe as a whole, but on a smaller scale. Inside the rings, at the center itself, there appears to be a void or empty space. As in the case of the universe as a whole, the galaxy is expanding but does not contain enough mass close enough together to reverse the present trend of expansion. Again, the hypothesis is put forward that the galaxy periodically expands and contracts in an unending series of 'explosions'.

Again, without any pre-conceived ideas about it, in both the case of the universe and the galaxy, matter appears to be created out of nothing. Either we cannot see the center due to inadequate technology, or the laws of physics as we now know them must be revised.

Our sun is undergoing a similar process on a smaller scale. On the surface of the sun matter is coalescing out of its most primary sub-atomic particles into protons, neutrons, and electrons which form the basic elements of hydrogen and helium. Scientists believe that at the center of the sun primary particles exist at tremendous temperatures and that the sun is an on-going 'explosion'.

Wherever matter is emitted – at the center of the universe, at the center of the galaxy, or in the sun – the process evolves from a void to sub-atomic particles, to protons-neutrons-electrons, to the primary elements of hydrogen and helium, and on to the more complex elements. It follows exactly the sequence described in the microcosmic world of matter except that it proceeds from the abyss downwards in reverse order.

As in the case of the quark theory, the hypothetical 'explosion' is more a thought about matter rather than what is actually observed. The word 'explosion' implies that matter existed prior to the explosion – which is the result of matter changing form. This way of describing it retains the assumption that matter is neither created nor destroyed. In spite of what is actually observed, science clings to the idea that something which appears to arise out of nothing must have come from something that existed before.

Again we arrive at the Abyss of the World of Matter. In both the microcosmic and macrocosmic views of matter, we reach the void at the source. Matter is being created out of nothing; this is the fact of observation, and not our thoughts about it. Because we cannot comprehend the evidence of our senses – that something is being created out of nothing – we are at a loss to explain the origin of either quarks or galaxies. Both views lead back to the Abyss. The Abyss is that point where both the laws of physics and our ability to conceptualize reach their limits.

The Nervous Observer

At the midpoint between the microcosm and the macrocosm is the observer. With his senses, and the help of his technology, he looks into the structure of the atom and out to the galaxies. His body is made of the same matter that he is observing; it contains traces of almost all the elements which make up the universe that surrounds him.

All sensation is a result of matter in the body interacting with matter in the environment. Although the matter in both cases is molecular in nature, the difference between them is this: the matter out in the universe is relatively unorganized while the matter in the body is highly organized – as organs of perception, a nervous system to process sensations and deliver their messages to a highly organized bio-computer, the brain. Sensation arises from the interaction of matter in the body with environmental matter on a molecular scale.

Sight occurs when the relatively unexcited cells of the retina are excited by incoming light. We do not see light itself which is not molecular in nature, but only the effect of light on the molecules of our retinas. Hearing is a specialised way of sensing air molecule pressure on the sensitive membrane of the outer ear. Touch is a more generalised way of sensing the pressure of molecules on the molecules of the skin. Smelling and tasting are the result of molecular scale reactions between chemicals in the body and chemicals in the environment. Temperature is the result of the different relative rates of oscillation between the molecules of the body and the outside world. Molecules which oscillate slower are sensed as being cold while those which move faster are hot.

Our experience of sensation, although it originates on the molecular level, is perceived on a level which is abstracted from the molecular by the structure of the nervous system. Each of the sense organs or pressure sensitive cells functions as a converter of molecular sensation into electrical impulses which are fed into the nerves. The nerve cells which receive the impulses from the sense organs or cells connect to an increasingly smaller number of neurons as the message is sent to the spinal cord and the brain. In this way thousands of impulses funnel into hundreds of nerve cells which funnel into tens of other nerve cells higher up, thus eliminating impulses and delivering an increasingly abstract impression of the original sensation to the brain.

The body, then, is a structural way of perceiving matter. The nervous system, by its very structure, creates a picture of the matter around us which is totally out of focus with the molecular level of events which gives rise to the picture. The picture we see of matter shows it to be solid and distinct from the observer, who is another solid piece of matter who ends at the skin where the 'outside world' begins. On the molecular level, however there are no such distinctions. All particles of matter interact molecularly and atomically with every other particle in the universe. If we could experience the matter in our bodies on a molecular level we would experience the activity of the whole universe. This is perhaps how a child experiences things until he is able to put the conventional picture together. People who gain sight later in life have to be trained to see things the way we consider the picture of things to be.

The brain forms the picture of reality by assembling the already muted and abstracted messages from the nervous system. The picture is put together from a combination of new, incoming sensation and previously-experienced sensation overlaid with the training and education about how to see new stimuli. The brain in some cases may choose to ignore some of the sensation and keep it unconscious according to the perceptual habits of the person.

But where is the observer? Is he his brain or is the brain, like his other organs of perception, part of the structural way he sees matter? For centuries, people have debated this essential point. At the level of the brain we again come to our thoughts about matter and not matter itself. For although the brain, as the rest of the body, is made of matter, it deals in thoughts which are not material in nature.

Those who have quieted their thoughts have found behind the almost constant chatter of thoughts and images of the brain a state of quiet, a kind of nothingness which is known as the void. When we look into each other's eyes we see a blackness at the center. The eyes, the windows to the soul, show us a picture of what lies beyond the brain, an empty void, the place where light comes in. In terms of our ordinary conceptual thinking who- or what-ever is the observer resides in the void of his own body, observing material forms which are apparently constructed from, and emerge out of, another void. Again, we arrive at the Abyss of the World of Matter.

The Abyss of the World of Matter

The Abyss has been approached from three directions: the microscopic structure of molecules, the macroscopic structure of galaxies, and the structure of the observer who exists on a scale midway between them. All three approaches have led back to our thoughts about matter. The search for the origin and nature of matter seems to end in the mind.

The Abyss, in this case, represents the boundary between mind and matter. The limits of the material world are, at the same time, the limits of our ability to conceive of something in our minds. The mind can only grasp what is between the limits of the infinitely small and the infinitely large. It can only contemplate what exists after it comes into existence and before it ceases to exist. Both mind and matter occupy the range between zero and infinity.

In the Qabalistic Tree of Life there exists a dividing line, called the Abyss, which represents the limits of both conceptual thinking and matter. It separates the first three Sephiroth of the Tree of Life called the Superiors, from the remaining seven Sephiroth, called the Inferiors.

In the world of matter the Abyss separates what is available to the extended senses (senses plus technology) from that which underlies and is the source of that which is being sensed. It represents a jump from physics, the science of physical phenomena, to metaphysics, the study of the first principles which give rise to physical phenomena.

Science cannot break through its own symbolism. Things are scientifically described in terms of what they are observed to do. If you ask a scientist what a thing is he will point to a set of symbols or equations which describe its observable behavior. The nature of the thing, to a scientist, is simply something which satisfies his equations. Due to the nature of science and its assumptions about what is real and what is speculation, it can never actually answer in a final way the question of what the thing is itself. What is it that the symbols and equations refer to? This question is not a scientific question. It is a metaphysical question.

The Abyss is the place where thought and matter are indistinguishable from one another. It is where being-ness and substance, ontology and physics, science and religion confront each other. Above the Abyss are the first three Sephiroth, the Supernals. They represent the basic nature and source of the seven Sephiroth below the Abyss, the Inferiors, which we have been discussing. It is in the Supernals that we must look for clues to the origin and nature of both matter and consciousness.

In order to understand the nature and origins of matter, the worlds above the World of Matter must be considered. The World of Matter is concerned with the structure and distribution of matter. The Worlds of Body and Mind are concerned with the perception and manipulation of matter. The World of Ability is concerned with the origin of both being and matter.

The Supernals

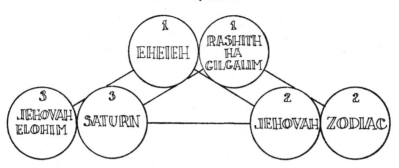

By placing the Supernals of the World of Ability next to the Supernals of the World of Matter certain analogies can be seen which give clues to the meaning of both worlds.

In the first chapter, entitled 'The Path of the Dot', the first Sephira to emerge out of Negative Existence is represented as a dot. Through the activity of the dot (representing the Creator) all the other Sephiroth came into existence. The first Sephira is the source of the whole of Positive Existence including the worlds of Ability, Mind, Body, and Matter. Another Sephira can also be represented as a dot. It is the first Sephira in the World of Matter.

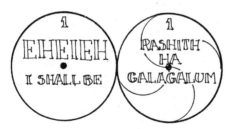

The name of God assigned to Atziluth (the World of Ability) is Eheieh, 'I shall be'. It indicates the ability of a God to be. The title assigned to the corresponding Sephira in Assiah (the World of Matter) is Rashith Ha, Gilgalim (or Galagalum), which is known as the 'Primum Mobile' or 'First Stirrings'. Both indicate becomings; one in the World of Ability, and one in the World of Matter. The dot which represents source is found in both the highest and lowest worlds of Positive Existence.

To continue the comparison of the worlds of Ability and Matter, an assumption must be made concerning the sequence of the second and third Sephiroth: In the realm of the Supernals there is no time factor. The second and third Sephiroth can be seen as having come into existence simultaneously. In the following, therefore, I have taken the liberty of reversing the order of the second and third Sephiroth in the World of Matter.

There is no precedent for this change in classical Qabalah. Some writers on the subject, however, state that the symbols assigned to the Sephiroth have been purposely mis-assigned to confuse all but the deepest initiates. I do not consider myself as having access to some knowledge unavailable to the rest of mankind. I am not an initiate. I have simply changed them because their new position yields some interesting insights and they seem to be more logically related than in their previous positions.

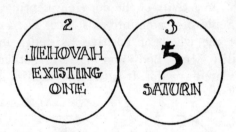

Jehovah, the name of God assigned to the second Sephira in the World of Ability is translated as 'Existing One' or 'Essence of Being'. It indicates, as has been stated before, the ability of a Creator to do. It is also the colloquial name of the Tetragrammaton which is a process of doing.

Saturn, the astrological symbol assigned to the third Sephira in the World of Matter, refers to individuality, aloneness, and control. The activity or doing-ness of an individual is common to both Sephiroth. The meaning of the symbol for Saturn is derived from the symbol itself (see Chapter Eight, Part Two, concerning the derivation of the meanings of the planetary symbols) and not the commentaries found in the astrological literature.

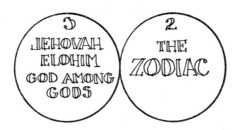

The name in the third Sephira in the World of Ability is Jehovah Elohim. It is in this Sephira that we find the key to the nature and origin of matter and consciousness.

We know from the preceding that Jehovah denotes the idea of an individual doer. Elohim, the remaining name, has been a topic of theological debate for centuries. Elohim is the name of God in Genesis who creates the world in seven days. Elohim is both male and female in gender and is *plural* in ending. Throughout the first chapter of the Bible, God continually refers to Himself as *we* or *they*. This has puzzled theologians for thousands of years. What could be meant by referring to 'The Only One God of Israel' as they? The Qabalistic literature translates Jehovah Elohim to mean 'God of Gods' or 'God among Gods'. Jehovah Elohim must be translated to mean, in this context, 'the activity of an individual God among other Gods of both sexes' or 'a relationship between Gods of equivalent nature'.

It is on this point that I depart from the cosmological model implied by Samuel Bousky (see Chapter Three, 'The Creative Law'). In Sam's opinion the name Elohim refers to the three primordial forces of the spiritual world which he calls the Life Force, Mind Force, and Soul Force. The ramifications of this departure from the commonly accepted way of seeing things by most metaphysicians will be apparent as the model of Psycho-metaphysics unfolds.

The corresponding Sephira in the World of Matter is the 'Firmament of the Fixed Stars' or the Zodiac. The Zodiac is the band of stars (suns) which surround our sun (star). The astrological symbol for the sun represents the true nature of the individual, his spirit or essential self. The symbol reminds us that our sun is not alone in the universe; it is a sun among other suns. We could say that the universe consists of a relationship between suns.

The names of God in the first world explain the symbols of the fourth world; the symbols of the fourth world clarify the meaning of the God-names. The Supernals of both worlds indicate the abilities of a God to be, do , and relate to other Gods. Since the Supernals are the source of the other seven Sephiroth, the World of Matter must be a result of a special *relationship* which exists between Gods.

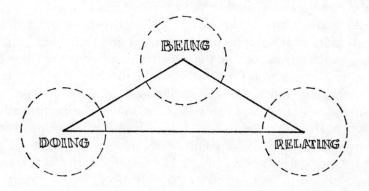

Some commentators say that the other Gods implied by the name Elohim are the Archangels who are like Gods with respect to men. Some suggest that they are forces by which the One God creates the universe. The psychometaphysical model, however, takes Jehovah Elohim literally to mean God among Gods of *equivalent* nature.

God's nature is described as follows: God is without prior source; He is eternally omnipresent and omnipotent; He exists above the confines of space-time; God creates the universe by emanating it from His being and He dwells within all its parts; His nature is inscrutable since it is beyond the capacity of the mind to conceive of Him and beyond the ability of the body to speak His name.

God is the Self of the universe. If there is more than one God, as the name Elohim implies, then each one is a Quantum God who is the Self of his own individual universe.

The Nature of the Self: The Quantum God

To understand the model of Psychometaphysics the reader must have a clear understanding of what I believe to be the nature of an individual. By individual, I mean the essential Self of the individual. The essential Self, or what might be called the trans-personal or spiritual self, is not just the body, mind, personality, or character structure. These are aspects of the Self which are no less real than the Self but, in this context, will be considered as functions or activities of the Self.

The Self is to be found conceptually in two frameworks. We can picture the Self as the center of being. Our picture might be one of a point or source from which the mind, body, and the physical universe are emanated and perceived through. Or, we can imagine the Self to be the whole *gestalt* of the individual including all facets of the individual in totality. Both of these conceptual viewpoints are useful – but the truth lies somewhere in between the two, and yet includes them both. In experience, the Self is beyond concepts of space and time.

The only real way of knowing the nature of an individual (your-Self) is to experience it directly (as in an enlightenment process such as the Enlightenment Intensive described in Part Three). For to describe the nature of the Self in words and con-cepts we would have to eliminate systematically all things which are not the essential Self and then, by intimation, say that what is left is it. This is basically the method of the Qabalah.

In the previous chapters concerned with Qabalah and the Creative Law the Self was described in various ways. Classically, the only essential Self described in the Qabalistic literature is a being we call God. All other Selves, including each of us, are seen as pieces of, or emanations from, God. In the first chapter, entitled 'The Path of the Dot', I took the liberty of symbolizing the Self of the Creator as a dot. The Qabalistic definition or description of God is much more wholistic: God is seen not only as a center but an infinitely large area. He is infinite and all powerful. His nature is inscrutable, i.e. cannot be comprehended with the mind of man. He himself is not physical but gives rise to all that is physical.

In the chapter entitled 'The Creative Law', we begin to see

that these same properties are to be found in each of us. The biblical statement that man is created in the image and likeness of God reinforces the idea that we have the same capabilities as God does, at least in potential.

Compare this with what the participants of the Enlightenment Intensive come up with in the deeper levels of their experience of self-enlightenment: 'I am God or God-like', 'I am the center of the universe', and so on. This again points to the nature of an individual as being much more than is commonly believed.

I would like to draw from some other sources which attempt to describe not the nature of God but the essential Self of every individual.

Gestalt Therapy, as developed by Frederick Pearls[15] makes no attempt to postulate a spiritual cosmology but makes some revealing assumptions concerning the nature of the individual. In Gestalt, the Self is seen in wholistic terms; that is, the whole individual, including his or her conscious and unconscious behavior, is seen as a whole organism functioning in the here and now. The therapy is based on the idea that whatever you are thinking or feeling is totally your responsibility and that you are doing it whether or not you believe you are doing it or not. This is important because most of us see our subconscious drives and behavior as being something apart from our 'real' selves. The process of growth or maturation, in Gestalt terms, is a process of owning all the parts of yourself, i.e. taking responsibility for the whole of you. Another insight of Gestalt is that you do not functionally end where your skin surface does, but that you are in process with the rest of the world. The boundaries that you draw around you mentally are purely arbitrary and depend on your particular character structure.

Carl Jung's picture of the nature of an individual points along similar lines. The Jungians see the evolution of man's consciousness as a process of individuation. As we evolve in consciousness, we become more and more 'individuated', or more of an individual with respect to the collective unconscious which binds us all together at our psychological roots. The picture is one of a central self which is emerging out of an essentially globally shared field of consciousness.

In the school of psychology called Psychosynthesis, as developed by Roberto Assagioli,[16] a clearer statement as to the nature of the self is given. The essential self that we are referring to is called the 'transpersonal self'. The transpersonal self is seen as being basically 'ontological'. *Onthos* means being, not process, and indicates something standing in itself. Although the self pervades the whole universe the self remains on its own level. 'In this same way the self is unchanging in essence, yet it sends out its energies, which are stepped down in intensity and transmitted through the superconscious (the field of the transpersonal self), and received, absorbed, and utilized by the personality . . .' And Jung says that archetypes and symbols (which are important elements of the superconscious) are transmitters and transformers of energies (from the self to the personality).

'The experience of the Self might be reached in the measure in which the "I" – which is a projection of emanation of the Self – ascends toward the Self, identifies with it, and is temporarily absorbed into it'[17]

A very poetic description of the Self can be found in Paul Foster Case's *The Book of Tokens*.[5] The first meditation (to be read in the first person) is on the first Tarot card, the Fool, which is a pictorial representation of the Self. It begins as follows:

> I am,
> Without beginning, without end,
> Older than night or day,
> Younger than the babe new-born,
> Brighter than light,
> Darker than darkness,
> Beyond all things and creatures,
> Yet fixed in the heart of every one.

> From me the shining worlds flow forth.
> To me all at last return,
> Yet to me neither men nor angels
> May draw nigh,
> For I am known only to myself.

Ever the same is my inmost being;
Absolutely one, complete, whole, perfect;
Always itself;
Eternal, infinite, ultimate;
Formless, indivisible, changeless.

It is the essential Self that I will now refer to as the Quantum God. The word quantum is to indicate that we are referring to a unitary, individual, essential Self. By the word God I mean the potentially infinite ability which *is* the essential Self (and for which there is no other word in English). I use the word God also because I intend to show that the essential Self of each individual is the same as that which we project into the world of our beliefs as an outside God. There is no outside God. But there are countless Quantum Gods. Each of them fills the description, both ancient and modern, of what God is conceived to be.

Your Quantum God is what you mean when you refer to your self as 'I', if you have not identified yourself as being your mind or body, energy or light, or any thing. The Quantum God is not a thing. It is your 'being-ness' itself.

The simplest and most accurate conceptualization of the nature of a Quantum God is Charles Berner's concept of infinite (not finite) ability: the true nature of an individual is ability; an individual does not *have* ability, ability is what an individual *is*. All other facets of an individual, including his thoughts, mind, body, and physical universe are demonstrations of the *ability-which-he-is*.

The Mystery of Negative Existence, The Home of the Quantum Gods

Positive Existence is Life in its broadest sense. It includes all states of being, activity, and relationship. Positive Existence is the state in which all things happen from the sub-microscopic world of nuclear particles to the infinite expanse of outer space. It includes all organic and inorganic phenomena on every scale. It includes the mind, body, and physical universe of every individual. What, then, is Negative Existence?

The classical way of conceiving of Negative Existence is that it is that which remains when every knowable thing has been removed. Called the Ayn Soph by the Qabalists, it is the 'Most Ancient of all Ancients'. Absolute and inconceivable, it is without essence, substance, or intelligence. It is symbolized by a circle which is said to contain a measureless domain of boundless infinity. It is the unconditioned state from which all things arise and to which they at last return.

Manley P. Hall, in his *Secret Teaching of All Ages*[8] describes it as follows:

> 'The circular shape given to Ain Soph signifies that space is hypothetically enclosed within a great crystal-like globe, outside of which there is nothing, not even a vacuum. Within this globe — symbolic of Ain Soph — creation and dissolution take place. Every element and principle that will ever be used in the eternities of Kosmic birth, death, and decay is within the transparent substance of this intangible sphere.'

Seen as a circle, the Ayn Soph is in a spatial context. Manley Hall adds:

> 'According to this concept, God is not only a Center but also an Area. Centralization is the first step towards limitation . . . When the consciousness of the Kosmic Egg (the Kosmic globe) is withdrawn into a central point it is called God, the Supreme One.'

Some Qabalists conceive of Negative Existence itself as God. The whole of Positive Existence is then seen as being emanated from it, as if it were a personality giving birth to all other personalities and things.

The psychometaphysical model takes a radically different viewpoint: Negative Existence is not a place or a being. It is the condition or state of all Quantum Gods who have not yet begun, or have ceased, to manifest themselves. It is a condition which has no space-time continuum; Quantum Gods exist there only as potentials. In this state, they are simply not doing anything, not even being. Each potential Quantum God is completely separate and discontinuous from all other potential or actual Quantum Gods (an actual Quantum God is in the state of becoming and is therefore in Positive Existence). Negative Existence is a state of absolute unconscious aloneness.

The closest Qabalistic equivalent to the idea of a potential Quantum God (as he exists in Negative Existence) is Adam Kadmon. Adam Kadmon is the name of the archetype of humanity. He represents the human to be, the image and likeness of God, in Negative Existence.

Negative Existence is not an abstract concept. It is the condition in which we all 'began', where we continue to live, and where we 'return' when we 'cease' to be. It can only be experienced in the deepest state of enlightenment, beyond the confines of the conceptual mind.

Emanation, the Specific Intentionality of a Quantum God

The central thesis and cornerstone upon which the Qabalistic cosmology is built is the concept of emanation. It states that the way, the *only* way, God does anything is through emanating from His being. The Sephiroth of the four Trees of Life are seen as representing God's emanations. The sequence of the Sephiroth are the sequence in which they are said to have emanated from God.

God is said to have emanated the first Sephira, Eheieh, directly from His abode in Negative Existence while all the following Sephiroth were emanated by Him *indirectly* from His occupation of the state of Eheieh. The process of emanation is not clearly defined in the literature but there are references to God's will as being His primary way of doing things.

From the Qabalistic references to emanation we might conceive of it as a mechanistic process. The picture it evokes is something like a light bulb (God) emanating light, or a transmitter sending radio signals in all directions. But the Qabalistic literature also states that God and His emanations are one and the same thing. Emanation is not separate from God as the light is a different thing from the light bulb. Emanation is the expression of God's very being-ness. What God is emanating *is* Himself. There is no mechanistic, conceptual model which can give us a clear idea of what emanation is. We must, therefore, look at it differently.

Let us consider the name God as indicating a personage rather than a thing (such as the universe as a whole) or a process (such as the Tetragrammaton). If we think of God as a person then emanation is simply God's will or intent. We can then define the nature of God to be intentionality or the ability to intend.

The central hypothesis of the model of Psychometaphysics concerning the Qabalah is this: the personage who is described in the Qabalah, Judaism, and Christianity as God is a metaphor for the essential nature of each individual human being. I am calling that essential nature the Quantum God. If this hypothesis is correct then every statement about God should be true about the nature of a Quantum God, in some analogous way.

Again, the psychometaphysical definition of the essential Self is that: a Quantum God is infinite ability; a Quantum God does not just *have* ability; ability is what, in essence, his being consists of. I realize that this is a difficult distinction to understand but, in my estimation, this is the closest conceptual equivalent to the truth of direct experience, achieved beyond the conceptual mind. (As experienced in the Enlightenment Intensive described in Part Three.)

This definition, arrived at through a radically different source, also fits the Qabalistic doctrine that God and His emanation are the same. If we accept the definition of God to be the ability to intend, then His emanation is His demonstration of His ability to intend. If a Quantum God is ability, then His primary ability, i.e. his emanation, is to intend.

I have used the word intend to distinguish it from the normal conceptualization of will. We know from the Process of the Creative Law that each of us is constantly creating thoughts, feelings, body, mind, actions, and circumstances. But most of us are aware that our creations are not always consistent with our conscious will. This is because we create our lives from a deeper, usually subconscious, source. This primal will, as distinct from conscious will, is the intent of the essential Self. Each of our personal realities find their source in the intent of the Quantum God within.

Your conscious will may or may not be, at different times, in harmony with your primal intent. When one's conscious will is out of phase with one's primal intent, an individual feels himself to be subject to fate, or may assign responsibility for his circumstances to an outside God. The process of personal maturation and growth can be defined as being the gradual making contact with one's primal intentionality, and bringing one's conscious will into phase with it. This is more a process of surrendering than it is of utilizing will.

To gain a clearer picture of the functioning of intent we must begin to see how it affects our thoughts, feelings, and actions. First, let us consider the nature of thought.

Our thoughts sometimes appear to come out of nowhere. But thoughts are reflections of our primal intent. The thoughts that just simply seem to happen to us are the results of mental patterns of thinking which are like engrained habit patterns. They arise out of our character structure, emotional reaction patterns in the body, and from the ability of the body to produce thoughts which are essential for survival such as thoughts of food when hunger arises. Most of us have a continual dialogue of thoughts with ourselves. These thoughts that just simply seem to happen to us are the results of mental rehearsals for some future event, or an on-going description in verbal thought concerning our perceptions of the present, or a mental conversation we are having with someone who is not present to talk to, or an attempt to integrate mentally some new experience or new information.

Some thoughts do not arise spontaneously but are the result of our conscious will. For example, if I were to ask you to have the thought of a house you could wilfully intend the thought of house to occur to you. Other wilful thoughts are produced when you are logically thinking something out or consciously solving a problem, writing a paper, or describing something to another.

Both modes of thought, spontaneous and wilful, contain two kinds of thought. The two kinds of thought, which make up all the thoughts that we are normally aware of thinking, are descriptive thoughts and opinions or considerations.

A descriptive thought is one which describes an object, situation, or idea. You may be describing something to yourself or another and you may be using words, symbols, or pictures of some kind to do so.

An opinionative thought is one which expresses your personal reaction, or opinion, or the way you have chosen to give consequence or meaning, or how you place emphasis or value on an object, situation, or idea. Your opinionative thoughts reflect your own character structure and how it reacts to the object of your thoughts.

These two kinds of conceptual thought are usually connected. Opinionative thought is often based on how a thing or situation is described and descriptive thought is often conditioned by one's opinion of the thing being described. We judge a person's objectivity by how little, in our opinion, his descriptions are determined by his opinions. The more opinions a person communicates, the more we, in our opinion, judge him to be subjective.

All conceptual thoughts have their source in another kind of thought, one which we are normally unaware of having. We are unaware of this kind of thought simply because it is not conceptual in nature and is preverbal. It is not mental in nature. Because this kind of thought has no conceptual content (it is not an idea, image, or concept) it tends to be hidden from awareness by the presence of the conceptual thoughts of which it is the source. I will refer to this primordial kind of thought as Thot. Berner calls it postulate thought ('thought' without the 'ugh'). Thot is identical to intent, the primary ability of the essential Self, the Quantum God. In Qabalistic terminology, Thot is to a Quantum God as emanation is to God.

You can consciously experience the functioning of your own Thot by simply pausing to contemplate how you create a wilful thought. If I suggest to you that you have the thought of a house in your mind you will find that you can easily produce an idea which to you represents a house. How did you do it? You simply intended to have it. It is your primary ability to do so. There is no process you go through to have a thought; you simply intend it into being as the Qabalistic God simply emanates things into existence. But the thought of house is a different thought than the thought of a tree or any other thought. Therefore your intent carries along with it specificness of intentionality which manifests as a specific thought, different from any other. So, Thot is a specific intentionality or a quantum (unit) of intent. What I have been describing is the active mode of Thot. Thot also has a passive mode.

Understanding something or knowing something, either through sensing, feeling, seeking, or hearing it, is conceived of generally as being a receptive or passive event. But how do you know something consciously? Certainly there is far more coming into our senses and perceptions than we can be conscious of at any one time. The only time you are conscious of knowing something is when you produce the Thot that it exists. You know something by having the specific Thot that it is known to you. What you know is entirely dependent on your intent to know. It is this intentionality, manifested first as Thot and subsequently as conceptual thought, which determines what you are conscious of and what you are not conscious of. This is the passive mode of Thot.

Conceptual thought is not the only manifestation of Thot. Thot also manifests in the body in the form of feeling and emotion. While emotion can be produced by a wilful intent as in the case of an actor who is playing a role, it most often is experienced as a spontaneous result of some interaction or situation involving others. These emotions are the response of our character structure to the situation at hand. When someone hurts us we get sad or angry or feel hurt before we can think a conceptual thought about it.

The character structure is just another construction of ours which puts certain patterns of response, both emotional and mental, on automatic pilot. It is based on previous experiences in life on which we have chosen, at the time of their occurrence, to base some behaviour pattern. The character structure functions as a memory bank computer whose main metaprograms have to do with survival and the behaviour in certain situations which will assure survival. It serves as a memory bank for what has been learned before. It would be somewhat tedious if we had to re-learn where to put our fingers each time we sat down to play the piano. In summary, the character structure is a memory of what Thots we have had in the past and have chosen to make a permanent part of our subconscious thought process.

If we temporarily eliminate the influence of the character structure, with its ability to evoke thoughts and feelings automatically, then we can see the effects of Thot in the body. Thot, the prime intentionality of the Quantum God, produces emotions and feelings in the body in just the same way that Thot produces thoughts in the mind. You can, through training, learn to produce emotion just as easily and directly as you produce thoughts.

Thot is the underlying intent behind both thought and emotion. It has both the qualities of emotion and mentality. In a fully integrated person, each thought has an emotional quality and each emotion has a conceptual counterpart. They have become two separate experiences in most of us simply because we, in the West, are more willing to experience and place a higher value on thinking rather than feeling. But we cannot really effectively separate them, even though we may believe that we are doing so. This is evident when we realize that our descriptive thoughts are inter-twined with our opinionative thoughts which are actually mental abstractions of our feelings about things.

In the Qabalistic metaphor, God emanates the four worlds of Positive Existence. In the metaphor of Psychometaphysics, a Quantum God creates, through utilizing his Thot, producing the existence and activities of his Self (World of Ability), his mind (World of Mind), his body (World of Body), and his physical universe (World of Matter). A Quantum God's Thot, seen as his basic ability, manifests in his mind as thought, in his body as feeling or emotion, and in the physical universe as matter.

To paraphrase the Qabalistic statement that God only creates or emanates the first Sephira, Eheieh, directly, and all the rest of the creation indirectly, we need only to consider what has been said about Thot. Thot is the only direct means by which a Quantum God does or knows anything. Thot belongs to the first World of Ability. All the other worlds are manifestations of Thot but are not pure Thot itself. In other words, the mind, body and physical universe are indirect creations which filter a Quantum God's direct experience with respect to his Thot.

Why should there be both a direct and an indirect process of creation and perception? Why is it that we must go through some kind of enlightenment process to experience things directly? The answer is found in the second major premise of Psychometaphysics: the universe is not the creation of a single God as all metaphysical systems and religions, both ancient and modern, dogmatically teach. According to Psychometaphysics, the universe is a co-creation which occurs between a multitude of God-like beings called Quantum Gods.

In this context then, a direct creative act or a direct experience only occurs between a Quantum God and his Thot. The indirect experience or creativity takes place in all other realms such as the mind, body, and physical universe since these realms are not the creation of one Quantum God but are also being created by other Quantum Gods. Thot is the direct expression of a single Quantum God, while the manifestation of Thot is an indirect expression of one Quantum God to another.

The first Sephira, in the Qabalistic system, is the only one which is considered to be a direct emanation from God. This Sephira, entitled Eheieh, denotes the prime ability of God to become. In the previous state, Negative Existence, God does not exist except as a potential individual. The potential is activated when God emanates His first intent and has the Thot that He exists. Once He exists He then can create the rest of Positive Existence. But since He does this from the secondary state of being, it is considered to be indirect with respect to His primary state in Negative Existence.

This is true for a Quantum God as well. Ridiculous as it may sound to the modern conceptual mind, a Quantum God comes into existence, as an individual, simply by intending to do so. He does so by having the Thot that he is. Once he has created himself (moved from Negative into Positive Existence) all his creations are actually co-creations which involve other Quantum Gods.

A Thot then is a Quantum God's primal intent. The first Thot that a Quantum God must emit in order to become a creator is the Thot that he exists. We can picture this occurrence graphically as an infinite domain of being-ness (symbolized by the dotted circle below) which suddenly concentrates itself into a point at the center of its former domain (the center point of the dotted circle).

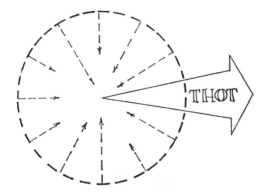

From within his new state of centeredness, a Quantum God can now emit further Thots. Each Thot is a unit of specific intentionality. Let us use a television picture tube as a model of what happens.

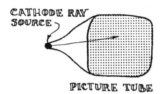

The Quantum God is represented as the cathode ray source within the picture tube. Each Thot that the Quantum God emits can be represented as a beam of light which hits the inside of the screen and causes a white dot to appear to the viewer. Each time the beam of light is emitted, it is directed at a different position on the screen. It lasts only long enough to produce the dot. Then the beam turns off and emits a new quantum of light in the next position on the screen. Within a very short time the light source has emitted bursts of light to all the available positions on the screen and has returned to its first position. The outside observer who is watching the screen does not see each individual dot but an entire picture produced by all the dots together. The phosphorescence on the inside of the screen holds the image of the dots until the beam has returned full cycle to produce a new image.

What, then, in the analogy of television, takes the place of the screen and its ability to attenuate all the discrete Thots that are emitted into a coherent picture? The screen, in this analogy, represents the functions of time, space, mass and energy. Before any Thot can manifest physically it must have a context in which to manifest.

How does God's intent or emanation become manifest as the physical universe? The Qabalistic literature tells us that God engraved His name and thereby formed the universe. The name, said to have been given to Moses by God, is the Tetragrammaton. Again, the Tetragrammaton denotes a process having the qualities of force, pattern, activity, and form. Let us assume that these qualities refer to four specific kinds of Thots or emanations.

ד	ה	ו	ה
TIME	SPACE	ENERGY	MASS

The first letter of the Tetragrammaton indicates force. Force indicates the activation or initiation of some occurrence or creation. Our definition of Thot itself satisfies this. One quantum of Thot can initiate a creation such as producing a thought in the mind but, to continue the existence of that thought, a series of Thots that it exists must occur. If more than one quantum of Thot that something exists is produced then the sequence of Thots introduces a new quality, time. Time is the effect of a continuous series of events. In this case, the events are Thots.

The second quality is pattern. This quality denotes structure. To have a structure there must be some shape or form. Patterns, forms and structures all have one thing in common. There must exist a separation between one point in the pattern and all the other points in the pattern. If there were no separation between one location in the pattern and another there would not be a pattern but only a point. If we look at the pattern as being a created thing which arises out of a number of discrete quanta of Thot, as in the television screen analogy, then the same Thot which creates pattern creates the condition we call space. Space is the Thot (the specific intention of a Quantum God) that some existing thing is located with respect to something else, or a part of a thing is in a different location from another part. Space is the Thot of located-ness.

The third letter indicates the quality of activity. Activity means motion. It suggests that something is travelling from one location to another. The specific Thot that there are locations to travel through is space. The specific Thot that a separation exists between these locations is the Thot which creates energy. Energy is the tension or potential which results when something is separated from something else. It is as if something which is separate from something else tends to reduce its amount of separation. It is held apart by the Thot of separation. Energy is the tension of separation. It is produced by the Thot of separation between locations.

The fourth letter of the Tetragrammaton denotes the quality of form. It is the result of the Thot of continuing is-ness which is time, the Thot that the is-ness is located which is space, and the Thot of the separation between locations, which is energy, all acting together as a unity. Form indicates, in this context, substantiveness or solidity. There is only one Thot lacking to produce a physicalness in which creation can take place and act as the the television screen acts in relation to the bursts of light which fall upon it. This quality is mass. Mass is not just a result of the previous three Thots which create time, space, and energy. It is another quantum of Thot. The Thot that the locations a thing can travel through are sequential is the Thot that creates what we call mass.

The letter *hay* is both the second and the fourth letter of the Tetragrammaton. The fourth letter indicates the second (pattern) carried into a formal structure. While the Thot that locations exist is pattern, the Thot that something travelling through those locations must follow a sequence of locations is mass. Mass is the orbit or path that something must follow to have solidity.

I have been talking about the qualities of time, space, energy and mass as they effect, the existence of some thing, or is-ness. These four qualities are the conditions under which some thing must exist to be part of the physical universe. That something is simply the Thot that a something or is-ness exists. In the television analogy, it is the burst of light that is projected into the context of the screen. In the model of Psychometaphysics, it is the Thot of the existence of some thing which is conditioned by time, space, energy, and mass. That thing is unconditioned matter.

But matter, as has been pointed out earlier, is not the product of one God, or Quantum God, but the result of a special relationship which exists between Quantum Gods. Here we must drop the analogy of the picture tube and begin the story of creation, a special relationship between essential Selves, the Quantum Gods.

6
The Co-Creation

The Paths of Two Dots

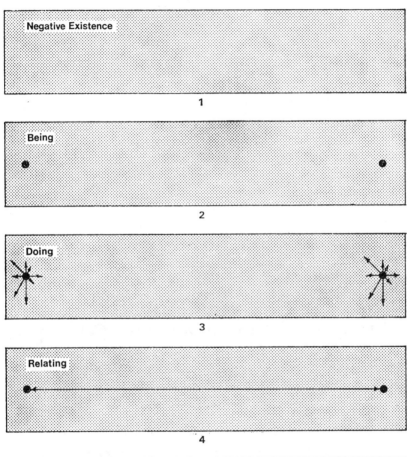

Negative Existence

1

Being

2

Doing

3

Relating

4

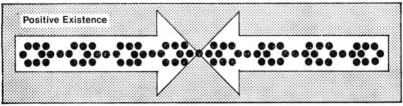

Positive Existence

5

The first chapter of this book, 'The Path of the Dot', is a graphic description of the emergence of the Creator out of the state of Negative Existence (represented by an infinite number of dots which occupy an infinite domain). In Negative Existence there remains any number of dots (representing potential Creators or Quantum Gods), each of which can, by the same process, become Creators.

The diagram on p. 125 parallels 'The Path of the Dot'. It is a graphic representation of what would happen if, instead of only one Creator, two Creators emerged into Positive Existence.

The rectangle at the top represents the state of Negative Existence. Each dot in Negative Existence represents a potential Quantum God.

Rectangle number 2 indicates the emergence of two Quantum Gods into the state of Being which is called Eheieh.

Rectangle number 3 represents the two Quantum Gods in the state of Doing called Jehovah.

Rectangle number 4 represents the two Quantum Gods in the state of Relating indicated by the name Jehovah Elohim.

Rectangle number 5 represents the creation of Positive Existence which results from the relationship between two or more Quantum Gods. Each of the Quantum Gods are emanating their own set of four worlds at each other. Notice that the tenth Sephira in their worlds of matter are common to both of them. The rectangle indicates that matter is created at the point of contact between Quantum Gods.

If, out of an infinite number of potential Quantum Gods, we take a look at just two, the creation of matter as a result of a special relationship between them can be described. Let us call them John and Martha.

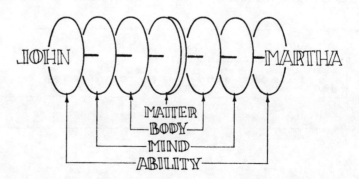

Here John and Martha are shown emanating their universes *at* each other. Their Worlds of Matter occur at the point of contact. Let us see what happens graphically if we add other Quantum Gods to their relationship:

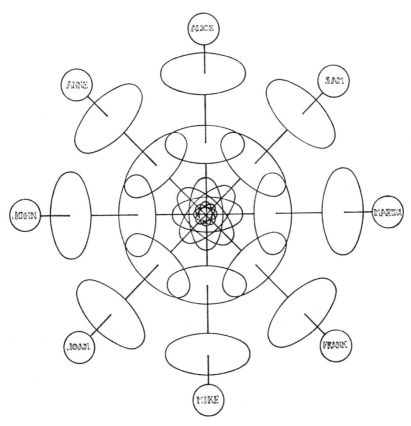

'Reality is a giant atom.' (Pierre Teilhard de Chardin)

These structural views of matter occurring at the point of contact between Quantum Gods does not, however, explain what matter is or how it came into existence. For this we need a more functional approach.

In the Beginning: The Story of the Co-Creation

The universe is as void. In this, the state of Negative Existence, the universe is without form, content, or being-ness. There exists nothing, not even a Thot.

Suddenly, without any sequence in time, two beings emerge. They are without form. They are beings of infinite ability. They have just begun to demonstrate their ability by emitting the Thot that they exist. We are calling them John and Martha and they represent any two Quantum Gods (regardless of the sex that their names imply).

'Potential John' becomes John by having the Thot that he is. John's Thot, 'I am', is his specific intentionality to be. In the act of having the Thot his nature is changed. John is. 'Potential Martha', by the sames process, becomes.

The Thot 'I am' is not only an intentionality to be. It is, simultaneously, the intentionality to contact another. By having the Thot 'I am' John brings himself into existence with respect to Martha. John and Martha are both *being* (by having the Thot 'I am'), *doing* (by having the Thot), and *relating* (they have become with the intent to contact each other).

One Thot is worth a thousand words. The Thot 'I am' includes the following: 'I intend to exist with respect to you (Martha).' We could, at this point, hypothesize that in order for John and Martha to come into the same universe they must emit some additional Thots such as 'Martha is' or 'We are'. But Thot has another aspect which has remained undefined up until now. Thot has been defined as a specific intentionality or quantum of intent. This definition holds true when we are talking about a single individual and his Thot. But here we are talking about two individuals and the Thot that occurs between them. In this case our definition of Thot must be extended. Thot can now be defined as a one-sided view of a communication between Quantum Gods. Our first definition does not change. To both John and Martha, their Thot is still their intent. But Thot would not occur to either John or Martha if each were absolutely alone in the universe. The state of being alone, in the absolute sense, is the state of Negative Existence in which no one exists with respect to anyone else.

For John and Martha to exist in the same universe with each other they must both have the Same Thot (intention). In having the same Thot, John and Martha are duplicating each other's intent. A duplicated Thot brings John and Martha into a common reality. They are now conscious of each other's presence.

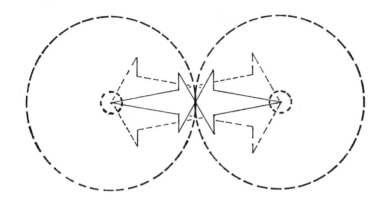

In the diagram above, the state of Negative Existence is represented by the white background which includes the diagram. The large dotted circles represent two Quantum Gods. The solid arrows indicate their mutual emanation of the Thot 'I am'. The act of emitting this Thot, each to the other, brings the Quantum Gods into being with respect to each other. The dotted arrows indicate the one-sided view that each would have as a result of them both having the same Thot, or intent. Each of them would experience a reflection of the other's Thot 'I am' (the dotted arrows). John would experience Martha's Thot 'I am' as if he were having the Thot 'She is' and vice versa. But they are the same Thot. The duplicated Thot occurs between them and places them in the state of becoming, called Eheieh, represented by the small dotted circles.

With the emanation of their first Thot a new element is introduced into the relationship between John and Martha, our two hypothetical Quantum Gods. Consciousness is a result of being in communication through the process of Thot duplication. Here I am not talking about normal waking consciousness in human beings, which I will refer to as awareness, but the most

basic, primordial kind of consciousness. This primary consciousness is the consciousness of direct experience, unconditioned by
the thoughts and feelings of the body-mind. In the state of Negative Existence there is no consciousness (no Thots are being
emanated). At the same time, however, the being-ness of a
Quantum God, while he is in Negative Existence, is infinite.
In moving into the first stage of Positive Existence (the state of
Being), being-ness is in the process of being limited while consciousness is, simultaneously, being expanded.

When a Quantum God emits a Thot he invests his infinite
being nature in it. Thot is an intent of his being and is composed of being-ness. Each Thot is a limited thing compared to
his being nature. So, at first, his conscious nature is very limited
with respect to his being nature. But the act of contacting another is a purposeful one. John and Martha are on the way to
building up a *consciousness* of each other's being natures. In
other words, their first duplicated Thot which made them conscious of each other's presence is the first step in a process of con-
sciousness-evolution, which is evolving toward the point when
John and Martha can be fully conscious of each other's (and
their own) being nature.

Their method of conscious evolution is the development of a
medium through which they can demonstrate their natures,
each to the other, and, at the same time, to themselves. The
medium is duplicated Thot, the only method they have to contact each other.

In summary, some important key ideas can be extracted from
the preceding;

1. Thot, in the active mode, is a quantum of specific intentionality to communicate something to another; Thot, in
the receptive mode, is a one-sided view of a communication
between two or more Quantum Gods.

2. Consciousness is the state of having a Thot which is
being duplicated by another individual. Consciousness arises
when two or more Quantum Gods are in communication
through Thot.

3. Reality is the result of Thot duplication between

Quantum Gods. The Thot of just one Quantum God would be unreal to any Quantum God who is not duplicating it.

4. Understanding occurs when the Thot of one Quantum God is duplicated by another.

5. Quantum Gods communicate with each other *only* through choice (Thot is intent).

6. The intent to become conscious of another, i.e. experience another, is love.

John and Martha are now in the state of becoming. Although they are both conscious that the other exists, neither of them is conscious of their own nature or the nature of the other. They are aware of each other's presence but nothing more. They cannot show themselves or demonstrate their ability to each other since their being-ness remains without limits and therefore has no differentiation or substantiality. They cannot even locate themselves with respect to each other. They must somehow limit and define their being-nesses in order to communicate further. They must begin to communicate in a particular (particle-like) way.

Matter is the Medium: Being is the Message

The Matter$_1$ Quantum

John emits the Thot 'It is'. Martha duplicates his Thot with her own Thot 'It is'. The duplicated Thot of is-ness creates primary matter (matter$_1$). Matter$_1$ is duplicated Thot. Primary matter is not a particle but singularity of being-ness, or a point of intersection between two or more Thots of it-is-ness. It occurs at the point of contact between Quantum Gods.

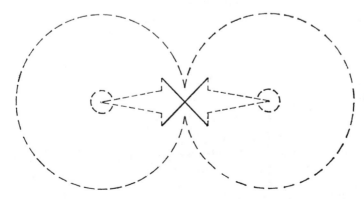

These two dotted circles represent the dimensionless domains of two Quantum Gods. Each of them is emanating the Thot of is-ness which creates matter$_1$ at the point of duplication (the intersection where the arrows representing Thot meet).

Since Thots are quanta, in order to continue the existence of their matter$_1$, John and Martha must emit a series of it-is-ness Thots, or emit a new Thot 'It exists'. The Thot that something exists (continuously) creates primary time (time$_1$).

Time

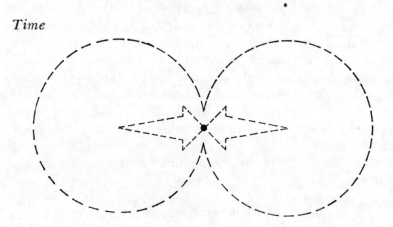

The additional Thot that matter$_1$ continues to exist has the effect of formalizing the existence of matter$_1$. It changes from a point of intersection to a matter$_1$ quantum, the basic building block of the physical universe. Although it is represented as a dot in the above diagram, it as yet has no dimensionality. In order to continue their dialogue and have a common domain in which to communicate to each other John and Martha must emit additional Thots *about* their matter$_1$ quantum.

Space

Primary space is created when John and Martha emit the Thot that a matter$_1$ quantum is located or has location. In order to locate something, additional points of reference are needed. The Thot of location expands the dimensionless matter$_1$ quantum into a three dimensional sphere of space (time is the fourth

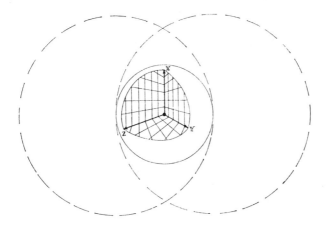

dimension). In the diagram above, the matter$_1$ quantum is both the center of the sphere and the whole sphere. The sphere of space acts as a common domain shared between the two Quantum Gods (dotted circles). The sphere of space has dimensionality but no fixed dimensions since it ranges from the infinitely small to the infinitely large.

At this point, John and Martha do not occupy bodies and are therefore also dimensionless. Later, the matter they use as bodies will define the midpoint between the infinitely small and the infinitely large.

Energy

In primary space, the matter$_1$ quantum exists in time$_1$ and space$_1$ but has no definite location within it. The matter$_1$ quantum occupies all positions in the sphere at the same time.

John and Martha emanate an additional Thot about its location. They emit the Thot that the locations which a matter$_1$ quantum can occupy are separate from one another. Since the matter$_1$ quantum is still in primary time (is-ness) the Thot would more accurately be described as 'the locations that a matter$_1$ quantum can occupy are separating.' The Thot that locations of a matter$_1$ quantum are separate, or are separating, creates energy.

The diagram above shows four probable locations of a matter$_1$ quantum. The separation creates a field of potential energy between them. The previous state (before locations were separate) acts as a ground state to the new situation in which locations are 'held apart' from one another.

Potential energy is defined as the energy a body has by virtue of its position. In a gravitational field a body gains potential energy by being lifted or separated from its zero state. Electrical potential is similarly created by exerting some effort to separate particles which, once separated, exhibit an opposite charge with respect to one another. If a conductor is placed between the charges they tend to reduce their separation and return to a non-electrical, neutral state. The work that the particles can do as they return to the zero energy state (non-separation) is measured as volts of electromotive 'force'.

We can conceive of the emanation of the Thot of separating locations as the work being done to create the energy$_1$ potential. We could say that John and Martha are 'holding things apart' with a blast of concentration. The potential energy$_1$ thus creted would return to the zero or neutral state if John and Martha ceased to emit the Thot of separating locations.

The Thot of separate locations quantifies the locations that a matter$_1$ quantum can occupy so that the sphere of space, once a homogeneous domain, now consists of discrete individual locations. Since the Thot occurs in time$_1$ and implies 'is separating' the sphere of space is now expanding; each location is separating from all the others. We can call these probable or potential locations which a matter$_1$ quantum may occupy at any given instant.

Each new Thot imposed on a matter$_1$ quantum by the Quantum Gods affects and is affected by the already existing conditions previously imposed. Time$_1$, the Thot of is-ness is changed by the Thot of separate locations into Time$_2$, discrete locations in time.

A matter$_1$ quantum can now occupy one location in one time.

This creates another kind of potential energy which results as the matter$_1$ quantum actually occupies one of its probable locations. The occupied location can be considered to be positive with respect to all unoccupied locations. All the unoccupied locations comprise the field of paramagnetic energy in which the matter$_1$ quantum moves. The matter$_1$ quantum in an occupied location would have electrical properties with respect to the paramagnetic (magnetic-like) field of potential locations surrounding it.

The Thot that locations are separating changes the picture of the space sphere. It is now a field of energy, composed of an infinite number of probable locations or quantum potentials, which is expanding.

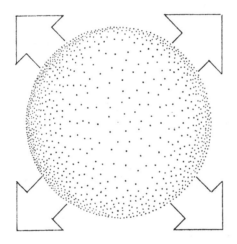

The diagram above shows the expanding field of energy which fills the whole sphere of space. The dots represent potential locations that a matter$_1$ quantum can occupy on the surface of the sphere. For simplicity, the lines of 'force' between the dots are not shown.

From inside the sphere things might look like this: The matter quantum appears at the center of the sphere; it disappears and reappears at some probable location within the volume of the sphere; it disappears there and reappears on the surface of the sphere. The matter quantum pops in and out of every location within the sphere and does it all at one time.

Mass

John and Martha each have the Thot that the locations that a $matter_1$ quantum can occupy are sequential. This Thot changes the highly random and indeterminate nature of the $matter_1$ quantum.

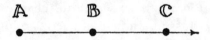

The Thot that locations of a $matter_1$ quantum are sequential creates the quality of matter called mass. It is a requirement that a $matter_1$ quantum, going from point A to point C, must 'travel' through point B (see diagram above). The matter quantum can no longer disappear at any location and reappear at another in a random fashion. It must now move through discrete locations in time and space. Mass and motion are two aspects of the Thot that locations of a $matter_1$ quantum are sequential. The $matter_1$ quantum now has a trajectory or path that it must follow.

The Thot of sequential locations affects time as well as space. Primary time ($time_1$) is simply undifferentiated is-ness. $Time_2$ is a unit of time analogous to an instant and indicates synchronicity (everything happening at once). Now, $time_3$ comes into being as a sequence of instants or a series of events in a continuum with respect to an observer. This is what we ordinarily call time.

Mass ties time, space, and energy into a Gordian knot. Space and time are now inextricably linked to each other as a $matter_1$ quantum must now move through increments in both. All the aspects of time, space, energy, and mass are integrated into new behavior patterns for a $matter_1$ quantum. The introduction of mass into the space sphere creates physical constants and laws which will be followed as matter evolves in complexity. The elements of motion, momentum, directionality and relative size came into being as aspects of the new order of things.

The matter$_1$ quantum is a true elementary particle. It has no internal structure. It gives rise to, but is not subject to, the known forces of physics. It therefore satisfies the criteria of the quark (see p. 96), the much sought-after cornerstone of the physical universe.

The Forces of the Physical World

The Relationship between Mass and Energy

Let us assume that the locations which a matter$_1$ quantum can occupy are evenly distributed throughout a non-expanding space. Let us assume further that we have a hoop or circle of fixed diameter and that we can place it over a cross-section of space. The hoop would overlay a certain number of locations which would fall on its circumference. The number of locations would be constant no matter where we placed the hoop. Now, let us place the hoop around a 'fixed' location in space and let space and the hoop begin to expand. The situation would look something like this:

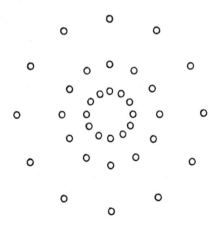

The small circles in the above diagram represent probable locations as space expands uniformly in time. Since the locations are non-dimensional points, they do not expand but as they move out from the center the distance between each of them and the center increases.

The velocity of a matter$_1$ quantum is constant, exceeding the 'speed of light' (see following description of light). Let us see what happens to the energy-mass characterstics of a matter$_1$ quantum as it is placed in orbit in one of the concentric circles of the diagram.

The amount of energy characteristic that a matter$_1$ quantum has is directly proportional to the distances between the positions that it is moving through. The amount of mass characteristic that a matter$_1$ quantum has is directly proportional to the number of positions that it travels through in a given period of time.

A matter$_1$ quantum moving in an outer orbit at a constant speed would exhibit more energy characteristics than one in a smaller orbit since the distances between the positions in a large orbit are greater. The same matter$_1$ quantum travelling in a small orbit would, conversely, exhibit more mass characteristics than one in a larger orbit because it would be travelling through more positions in an equivalent period of time.

If a matter$_1$ quantum were to change from one orbit to another, its mass-energy characteristics would change accordingly. A matter$_1$ quantum jumping from a larger orbit to a smaller orbit would shed some of its energy characteristics and take on more mass characteristics.

Thus mass and energy are convertible factors. They are not really two different things but two aspects of the conditioned behavior of a matter$_1$ quantum.

Let us assume that the mass and energy characteristics of a matter$_1$ quantum tend to stabilize at some distance from a hypothetical center around which it is orbiting. We can imagine this as happening in one of two ways; the matter$_1$ quantum is simply orbiting its center at a fixed distance forming a shell around its center; or it might oscillate from its center, filling the space between the center and its outermost shell. In the second case it would spiral outward to its orbit of stability and back again to its center.

The path of the matter$_1$ quantum might look like this:

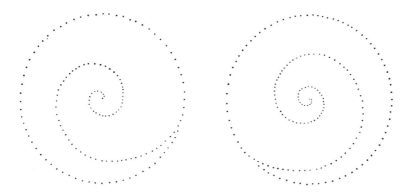

The matter$_1$ quantum would appear to spiral out from center to an outside observer. The direction of spin would be determined by the velocity and proximity of other matter$_1$ quanta in the sphere of space.

As the matter$_1$ quantum spirals out from center it will reach a distance from the center where its energy and mass characteristics are balanced with its space-time context. The matter$_1$ quantum would then be occupying the first quantum shell. In order to conserve its momentum it must begin to spiral inward again. The matter$_1$ quantum is now an oscillating spiral with respect to a 'fixed' center. Since the center is moving as well as the matter$_1$ quantum, the spiral is not flat but is stretched out in space and time to form a vortex. The vortex formed by the outward spiralling is balanced by the vortex formed by the inward spiralling. Since the double vortex is held within the quantum shell it takes the form of a sphere whose surface is described by the expanding and contracting spiral path of a matter$_1$ quantum.

The Sub-atomic Particle

The motion of a spiralling matter$_1$ quantum describes a sphere with respect to an outside observer moving at a slower speed.

The non-dimensional matter$_1$ quantum is now forming a particle of matter, a wave packet of matter, perhaps what we call a sub-atomic particle. From the outside, the observer sees a particle and not the matter$_1$ quantum which creates the particle. This is because his rate of observation is in sequential time (time$_3$), while the matter$_1$ quantum itself remains in time$_1$.

The quantum shell it occupies defines the size of the particle as well as its mass-energy characteristics. The shell is a circumference which intersects all probable locations at which the mass-energy characteristics of a matter$_1$ quantum tend to be stable in a particular location in space.

At some point within a particular observational context, the wave packet would stabilize for a period of time, forming the first harmonic or first quantum shell. It would then be forming something like a three dimensional standing wave with respect to the observer. It would then act as a primary particle in interaction with others of its kind.

The domain the wave packet-particle occupies (its volume), its mass-energy characteristics, frequency, wavelength, amplitude, spin, relative polarity (or charge), are dependent on the proximity and configurations of all other particles in the space sphere and the influence of the technique and equipment used to observe it.

Under special circumstances, collisions may occur between symmetrical pairs of wave packet-particles which force them both to revert to their original state as matter$_1$ quanta. This gives rise to the observed phenomenon of particle-antiparticle annihilation.

The Strong and Weak Nuclear 'Forces'

We must also take into account the fact that all particles are affected by all other particles. To add to the complexity of the situation consider that a particle can be spiralling in one of two directions, its motion with respect to other particles can be taking place at differing directions and speeds, its axis of symmetry can be at any angle, and it may spin around its axis while it moves in any orbit. In addition, orbits would be distorted into ellipses. All these permutations have their effects on the behavior of particles and this gives rise to the complex nature of sub-atomic physics.

Particles occupying quantum shells near the center act relatively strongly with each other. They would also contain more mass characteristics than particles occupying shells further out. These effects are referred to as the weak and strong nuclear 'forces'. They are not forces at all, but the result of the space-time geometry already described.

Electrons are particles which occupy relatively large orbits with respect to the nucleus. Their orbits are ten thousand times more distant from center. They therefore have less mass and are less tightly bound to the center of the atom than the particles in the nucleus. Electrons are the outermost elements of a compound particle and their orbits define the size of the next order of magnitude in particulate matter, the atom.

The Atom

The simplest atom is hydrogen. It has one particle in a small orbit and one in a large orbit.

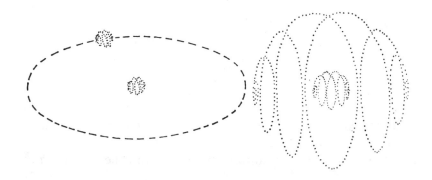

The diagrams (p. 141) show two possible configurations of an atom of hydrogen. The other atomic elements have additional nucleons and electrons which occupy more and more quantum shells, near center in the case of nucleons, and far shells in the case of the electrons. The number of nucleons (protons and neutrons) in the nucleus is directly related to the number of electrons an atom has. The activity of mass and gravity in the nucleus determine to a great extent the activity of the electrons.

The Particle versus the Wave

The spherical shape is generated by the assumption that the particle is in motion. To an observer who is following alongside at the same, or faster, speed, it would appear as an oscillating spiral. To another observer who is relatively farther away, or moving slower with respect to it, it would appear as an oscillating sphere or field whose changing diameter would describe a wave in space:

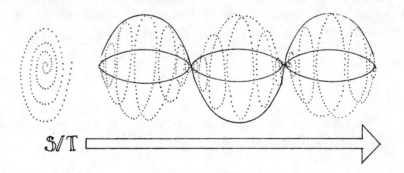

Particles of matter exhibit both particle-like and wave-like behaviour depending on the point of reference of the observer.

The effects of time-space-energy-mass which change the $matter_1$ quantum into a particle of matter bring us to a new scale of things in the sphere of space. The new order of magnitude arising from particulate matter changes the focus of John and Martha's consciousness as well as the interactions that take place between particles.

While the $matter_1$ quantum could exist in $time_1$ (is-ness) and time$_2$ (instantaneousness), the particle only exists in time$_3$ (sequential events). The matter$_1$ quantum could travel at infinite speeds while the particle is confined to speeds less than the 'speed of light', the conversion factor between time$_1$, time$_2$ and time$_3$.

Temperature

Matter$_1$ quanta in the same space sphere instantaneously (time$_2$) affect each other's relative positions and energy-mass characteristics, irrespective of their distance from one another. Particles, however, affect each other in proportion to their distances, directions, and velocities. The relative rates of oscillation between any two particles is called temperature. Temperature is defined as the relative amounts of kinetic energy a particle has, whether it is a simple particle like a neutron or a complex particle such as an atom or molecule. The greater the difference between their relative rates of oscillation, the greater the difference in their temperature. The faster rate is considered to be hot with respect to the slower rate.

Speed of light

A change in the rate of oscillation of one particle will effect a change in the rate of the other particle. On the scale of the matter$_1$ quantum the change is instantaneous. On the scale of particles the change will appear to take place at the 'speed of light'.

Let us assume that one of the two oscillating particles is located in the retina of an observer's eye. His viewpoint then exists in time$_3$ and he is looking at the other particle through the lens of the particulate order of magnitude (on a molecular scale). Since he is out of focus with respect to the underlying matter$_1$ quanta which produce the molecules, he does not 'see' matter$_1$ quanta but only the molecules they produce. Any change in the particle he is observing will cause a change in the particle in his eye. What he experiences, as the relative temperatures of the two particles change, will be slowed down further since it will take some time for a change in his retina to reach his brain. When the change is registered he may imagine that some energy has travelled from the particle he is observing to the particle in his eye. He might call this apparent transmission of energy 'light' or some frequency of 'electronmagnetic radiation'.

Since his body is not sensitive enough to measure the whole range of radiation or its speed, our observer would naturally turn to his instruments. Through his technology he would find that 'light and all frequencies of electromagnetic radiation' travel at the same 'speed', no matter what the speed or direction of their source is with respect to him. But since whatever technological device he 'measures' light with is particulate in nature, he would still be observing the phenomenon through the lens of particulate matter. He can never see that light is a result of the instantaneous change between all matter$_1$ quanta. The 'speed' of light is then a constant factor between the rate at which he can observe things through particulate matter, and the rate at which things actually occur.

Although this rate remains constant (instantaneous), the frequency and wave lengths vary with the location, speed, and configuration of the particles in question. Frequency and wavelength are the various ways in which matter$_1$ quanta affect the instruments.

Gravity

It was the discovery of this upper limit to the speed of particulate matter which led Einstein to formulate his theory of relativity. His conception of gravity fits well with what we are talking about. It can be described as a function of the properties of the space-time field that created particulate matter. Here we must look at its effect on two or more particles interacting in the sphere of space.

As was shown earlier, the amount of mass a particle has depends on how many locations it passes through in a unit period of time. Let us assume that we are inside a particle travelling with uniform velocity (constant speed and direction). Our mass would remain constant and we would be floating around the inside of the particle experiencing zero gravity as in free-fall. If either the direction or the speed were changed we would experience a change in our mass, and would find ourselves pressing up against one of the sides of the particle. Since we cannot see out of the particle to know that our motion with respect to some outside point has changed, we might say to each other that we are experiencing gravity. We would notice that our experience of mass, in the form of momentum, and gravity are directly proportional to each other.

All motion is relative. In the curved space of our space sphere all motion is orbital. The smaller the orbit is, the more this is apparent. What appears to be motion in a straight line is simply motion in a large orbit observed in a small segment.

Our particle is, then, moving around some center point. Our experience of mass and gravity is proportional to the size of our orbit and the speed at which we travel on it. The gravity we experience is simply the effect of our relative motion with respect to the center we are orbiting. If, however, we were suddenly to claim that our particle is at rest with respect to the center we are orbiting, then the center would appear to be orbiting us. Since we are still experiencing gravity, we might conclude that gravity is a property of mass, or, if we could connect the motion of the center with our condition, we might conclude that the movement of the center around us is creating a gravitational field in our vicinity.

Relative time

This relative motion also affects time$_3$. Time$_3$ is a sequence of events. If we consider the locations we pass through as events in time, then we can see how mass, gravity, and time are related. If we accelerate by increasing our speed then our mass and experience of gravity will increase. The number of locations we pass through in a unit of time will increase as well, so our clock, which measures locations as it ticks, will speed up. But since all processes within our accelerating particle speed up at the same rate, our rate of observing the clock will speed up accordingly. The net effect will be that our clock will appear (to us) to be ticking at the same rate as it was before we accelerated.

The same would be true if we went to the center of the orbit with a similar clock, since the center would be accelerating in the opposite direction relative to our previous position. At both positions, our clock would appear to be running at a constant rate. But the center is also orbiting some third point in space which is *its* center. If we could observe both clocks from this new center, considered to be at rest with respect to the orbiting first center and its orbiting particle, then we would see time differently. It would appear that the clock in the particle is ticking slower than the clock at the center of its orbit. This is because the rate at which an observer at rest 'sees' the clocks is slower than the rate of observation of the observers moving with the clock.

To summarise, all the so-called 'forces' of the physical world can be seen as the ramifications of the Thots that John and Martha, our hypothetical Quantum Gods, are having about the matter$_1$ quantum. The strong and weak nuclear forces, the electromagnetic forces, and the force of gravity, are not forces at all but manifestation of a matter$_1$ quantum in the curved space-time continuum which is the common domain of inter-action between Quantum Gods.

Evolution

If we could stand outside the universe, as in the state of Negative Existence, and watch the co-creation of matter and consciousness as it has been described we might see the follow-ing: out of the limitless and boundless void there suddenly emerges a tremendous amount of high temperature sub-atomic and atomic matter and energy. This description fits both the observed phenomena of astrophysics and the tale of John and Martha, our two hypothetical Quantum Gods. It is the 'Big Bang'.

Billions of years, *of our time*, later we find ourselves in a universe full of stars. Each star is emanating its light to all the other stars just as all Quantum Gods emanate themselves at all other Quantum Gods.

On another level of activity, millions of years further along, the earth is formed along with other planets due to the inter-action of one star upon another. The earth cools. Its environ-ment allows for the 'complexification' of inorganic matter into the emerging forms of life that we are all familiar with. In the last few seconds, with respect to the eons that preceded it, a life form emerges which is superior in survival to all the others. It takes dominion over the earth. It is Man. The Quantum Gods have arrived.

The purpose of evolution is this: the Quantum Gods have created matter in order to contact and become conscious of each other and themselves. A major step along the way to fulfilling that purpose is the creation in matter of the material equivalent of their nature as beings of infinite ability. To paraphrase the Bible, a Quantum God creates an image and likeness of himself in the World of Matter. His image and likeness is his body.

We think of evolution in terms of eons of time. We cannot really conceive, with our limited conceptual minds, of the eternity that it must have taken for the universe to evolve from the Big-Bang to the present day. The scale of time involved is astounding. Yet a Quantum God exists outside time. He lives only in the eternal now. To him all of creation takes place in less than an instant. From his vantage point in Negative Existence, time is no more than a Thot he is having. Seen in this way, evolution is no more than a mental construct of the time-bound conceptual mind. Both the past and the future are no more than mental projections.

The description I have given of the co-creation is no more than a parable. There is, in fact, no creation at all. The entire physical universe, including the bodies inhabiting it, is simply a relationship between all the Quantum Gods participating in it. The forms which matter appears to take, their evolution, and their reproduction after their own kind, are experienced as they are because that is the way we mentally are able to deal with it. The way things are is a reflection of the state of consciousness we have achieved which, in turn, reflects the degree to which we are willing to experience each other as Quantum Gods. At some further point in the development of our relationship (as expressed by the physical world) we shall experience ourselves, the world, and others in a different way. Some day the physical world will have served its temporary purpose. It will then dissolve like a dream we once had. Then we shall be experiencing ourselves and each other in a more direct way, without the need to place matter and mentality between us and the direct experience of ourselves.

For the time being matter is serving its purpose as a means of communication. The parable of creation must, for the present, continue.

Matter is composed of the inter-related consciousness (duplicated Thots) of the Quantum Gods. As matter 'complexifies', consciousness 'complexifies' with it. Matter evolves out of the matter$_1$ quanta into sub-atomic particles, nucleons, atoms, molecules, megamolecules, life-forms, and so on. Quantum consciousness (Thot) evolves into particulate consciousness, atomic consciousness, and so on. Each level or state of evolution has its type of consciousness. All things in the universe are composed of consciousness.

A rock has rock consciousness as a tree has tree consciousness. All things whether we consider them to be dead or alive are expressions of the consciousness which informs them. The shape, color, texture, weight, taste and smell of any object is its communication to the world of its mode of consciousness, expressed uniquely by each individual thing. The universe constantly expresses the uniqueness of each thing within it while, at the same time, demonstrating the unitary nature of substance itself.

At the vanguard of evolution is the human body. It too expresses the consciousness which informs it. It is the most highly complex of all nature's productions. It contains all the naturally occurring elements of the universe. It is a microcosm of the universe as a whole. It expresses all the previous stages of evolution from the molecular through the cellular up to the primate, as one statement in time.

The human body, as far as we know, is unique among all the forms of the physical world. It is the only form which is able to contemplate its own existence. It is the only form which has a being-ness in it which is able to transcend the physical world in such a way as to be able to look back upon itself and the world, as subject looks back on object. It is the only material form in our present stage of evolution which exemplifies in matter the quality of infinite ability. Humans are like Gods with respect to all other material forms.

The human body is a direct expression, in the World of Matter, of the nature of a Quantum God. It is his means of being in the physical world and of expressing his being-ness to others. It is his means of communication and action. A Quantum God is at once not his body and, at the same time, is his body. His body is his expression of himself so that the way his body functions, its state of health, its flexibility, its ability to do things and communicate, its capacity to think and feel, and its aliveness, reflect directly the nature and condition of the Quantum God within. And yet a Quantum God is more than his physical body.

Here we must jump to the Worlds above the World of Matter to see what aspects of a Quantum God's nature are expressed in his bodily existence. But these worlds are not above the bodily world as we might think of heaven being above earth; they are contained within the World of Matter and function, so to speak, behind it. It is all happening at one time and one place. In the realm of the body, the Worlds of Ability, Mind, Body, and Matter function as an inseparable unity.

7
The World of Ability

The basic, intrinsic ability of a Quantum God is to emanate a Thot. A Thot, as has been stated, is a specific quantum of intentionality which arises when a Quantum God intents to be, do, or relate in some way. There is no mechanism or process involved in the having of a Thot; it is a direct expression of the nature of a Quantum God as infinite (not finite) ability.

The World of Ability, then, indicates ten basic modes or categories of Thot production. The Qabalistic literature indicates that 'They are ten and are without number.' This indicates that there are an infinite number of possible Thots which a Quantum God can have but that they fall into ten basic categories or types which are symbolized by the ten Sephiroth of the Tree of Life.

We have suggested that, at the allegorical level of the Bible, all the names in scripture are codified formulas for states of consciousness. This is also true of the ten names of God which are assigned to Atziluth from which the World of Ability is derived.

When a Quantum God has a Thot the very act of having that Thot places him in the state of consciousness defined by that Thot. When a Quantum God has the Thot 'I am', he is demonstrating his ability to be, and is in the state of conciousness of Being. Similarly, when a Quantum God has any Thot other than the Thot 'I am', then he is demonstrating his ability to do and moves into the state of Doing. When a Quantum God has a Thot which is duplicated by an identical Thot from another Quantum God then he is demonstrating his ability to relate (or co-create) and is in the state of Relating. This, as has been pointed out, is the meaning of the first three Sephiroth of the World of Ability.

The Supernals

The first three Sephiroth, representing the basic modes of Being, Doing, and Relating, are the basic modes of Thot production from which the remaining seven Sephiroth are derived. The first three Sephiroth, the Supernals, are so archetypal that there is no real difference between the ability that they indicate and the state of consciousness that they represent. In the inferior seven, however, the abilities indicated and their resulting states of consciousness become more differentiated. In the World of Mind and World of Body these differences will become even more apparent.

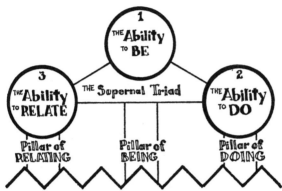

The Supernals are the capitals of the three pillars of the Tree of Life, called Qabalistically, from the reader's viewpoint, the Pillar of Severity on the left, the Pillar of Mildness in the middle, and the Pillar of Mercy on the right. For the purpose of this discussion, I will re-name them to conform with the name of the Sephira at the top of each pillar: on the left is the Pillar of Relating, in the center is the Pillar of Being, and on the right is the Pillar of Doing.

The Ontological Mind Triad

The Supernal Triad is separated from the Inferiors by the Abyss. In the World of Ability, the Abyss divides the three primary modes of Thot from their manifestation in the seven Sephiroth of the Inferiors. The first three Sephiroth of the Inferiors are reflections of the Supernals in the realm I shall call Ontological Mind. Ontological means of, or pertaining to, exist-ing-ness or being. Mind, in this context means a patterning or structuring of Thot.

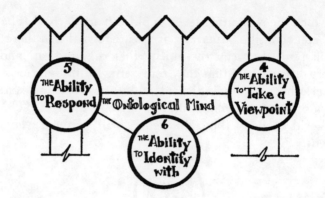

The fourth Sephira bears the name, El. This name of God was decoded by Samuel Bousky to indicate the idea of Force. (see Chapter Three)

In the context of this model, Force is the same as the ability to do. It sits on the Pillar of Doing and corresponds with the state of Doing as it manifests in the Ontological Mind.

This, the first Sephira of the inferiors, indicates the manifestation of Thot emanation (doing) in the context of space-time. While the Superiors are outside time (above the Abyss), the Inferiors are not. In the Superiors, a Thot is a unique event which is unconnected to any other event and has no duration in time. Each Thot occurs at the instant it is emitted by a Quantum God and ceases to exist when he ceases to have that Thot. In the fourth Sephira and all succeeding Sephiroth, however, Thot has duration.

In the second Sephira, a quantum of intentionality produces a Thot. In the fourth Sephira an additional quantum of intentionality is attached to the first Thot. This additional Thot is an intentionality that the first Thot continue to exist beyond the instant of its creation. Thot is the intention 'It is'; thought is the intentionality of 'It continues to be'. Thot, in the fourth Sephira, is transformed into thought.

In the realm of the Superiors (outside time) a Quantum God can have any number, or any kind, of Thots. Similarly, in the Inferiors, a Quantum God can have any number, or any kind, of thoughts. In the Ontological Mind Triad, however, we are concerned with a particular class of thought. Ontological thoughts are not thoughts about things as such. An ontological thought is more a statement about how something is to be seen. It is an attitudinal viewpoint which acts as a point of reference from which all further thoughts are created and experienced. These attitudinal viewpoints do not affect the things of the material world but instead affect the way a Quantum God perceives them.

An ontological thought is an intentionality of viewpoint. Just as the Thots of time, space, energy, and mass condition matter, ontological thoughts condition the consciousness and state of being of the Quantum God who has them. An ontological thought is an attitude fixed in time. It is a lens through which a Quantum God will see all succeeding thoughts and feelings. Ontological thought literally stands between a Quantum God and his body. Through the use of ontological thought he can limit, condition, and eliminate from his own subjective awareness any information which his body gives him which he is unwilling to experience. Ontological thought is the basis of the subjective mind.

The fourth Sephira represents the ability of a Quantum God to take a viewpoint which then becomes his fixed mental attitude in the World of the Mind.

The fifth Sephira bears the name Elohim Gibor. Elohim indicates a relationship between Quantum Gods. Gibor means power or might. The name indicates the power or effect that relating to others has on a Quantum God. Since we are looking at the Tree of Life as a representation of the abilities of one Quantum God, the fifth Sephira indicates the ability of a Quantum God to relate or respond to another Quantum God through the medium of ontological thought (the fifth Sephira emerges from the fourth).

The fifth Sephira represents the primary function of attitudinal viewpoints taken in the fourth Sephira. Since a Quantum God is participating in a relationship with other Quantum Gods, he is subject to the effects that others have on him. There is nothing in life that affects an individual more than his relationship with others. Others are at once his source of consciousness and fulfilment and the major threat to his well-being. By participating in life with others he is limiting his nature as an omnipotent being. He retains the quality of omnipotence by exercising his ability to determine, to some degree, how he will experience life and others. He does this through the taking of fixed attitudes towards what he is experiencing. These attitudes tend to isolate him from the effects that others have on his experience. By taking an attitude he is eliminating from his own awareness all but what he chooses to experience and be aware of. In this way he retains a degree of omnipotence.

Yet it is these fixed attitudes which limit a Quantum God's ability to respond to others. Each attitude is a statement of 'I do not want to think or feel this.' Whatever area of his relationships with others that that attitude encompasses will, as a result, be restricted in terms of his ability to think and feel in that area. The more attitudinal viewpoints a Quantum God has within his character structure the more he is separated from the direct experience of his body and, in turn, others. The more attitudes he has, the more restricted is his capacity to respond.

The sixth Sephira bears the name, Eloah Vadaath. Eloah is the singular feminine form of the name Elohim and indicates a single Quantum God. Vadaath has to do with the attainment and utilization of knowledge and experience. It sits on the Pillar of Being in the realm of Ontological Mind indicating a state of being identified with the mind or mentality (thought). It indicates the ability of a Quantum God to perceive and act through the Ontological Mind, i.e. actually identifying himself with his mind, and becoming one with it.

Dion Fortune, in *The Mystical Qabalah*,[2] assigns the sixth Sephira the title 'Tetragrammaton Eloah Va Daath' and interprets it to mean 'God made manifest in the sphere of the mind'.

From his state in the sixth Sephira, a Quantum God is able to control what he perceives (through the establishment of attitudinal viewpoints in the fourth Sephira) and consequently control his response (the fifth Sephira). The Ontological Mind triad is operated from the sixth Sephira which represents a Quantum God's ability to mediate, utilize, and control his subjective awareness.

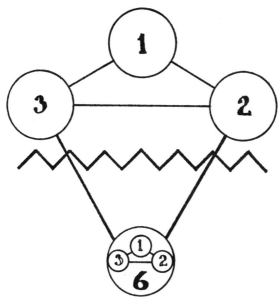

The sixth Sephira is also the apex of a triangle (pointing down) connecting it with the second and third Sephiroth. This triangle connects the Supernals with the sixth Sephira, thereby crossing the Abyss as no other triad in the Tree of Life does. To me, this indicates that the first three Sephiroth are incorporated into the sixth and lie behind it. It indicates the incarnation of a Quantum God into the central position of the Body-Mind from which all succeeding experience and activity can be experienced and controlled.

The Corporal Mind Triad

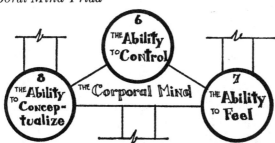

The Corporal Mind Triad consists of the sixth, seventh, and eighth Sephiroth. In this Triad the sixth Sephira represents the place from which the Quantum God takes in experience and information and initiates activity through the remaining lower Sephiroth. The sixth Sephira is the connecting point between the subjective mind (Ontological Mind) and the perceptions of the body as manifested in the brain (Corporal Mind).

The seventh Sephira bears the name Jehovah Tzaboath. Jehovah is the colloquial name for the Tetragrammaton. Tzaboath is translated as 'of Hosts'. A host is someone or something which supports the existence of another. The name suggests some function which supports the existence of the creative process (Tetragrammaton) in the realm of the Corporal Mind.

The seventh Sephira represents the ability of a Quantum God to feel and emote through the transmutation of energy. He does this through the utilization of his body. His body enables him to contact the energy aspect of the universe surrounding him. Since we are discussing the Corporal Mind we are here referring to a Quantum God's subjective experience of his emotions and his ability to influence them.

The eighth Sephira has the title Elohim Tzaboath. Again, Elohim is a relationship between Quantum Gods. Tzaboath, as we know from the previous Sephira, means something which supports the existence of something else. It indicates a function of the Corporal Mind which supports the existence of relationships. Since we are talking about mentality, which is the way a Quantum God controls subjective experience, this Sephira indicates the ability of a Quantum God to translate sensual and emotional experience into mental images or thoughts. It is the ability to conceptualize, or symbolically represent intentionality and experience in thought.

The ability to conceptualize is related to the ability to take an attitudinal viewpoint, indicated by the fourth Sephira of the Ontological Mind Triad. The difference is this: The fourth Sephira indicates the ability of a Quantum God to affect his state of being (ontology) by taking a mental stand in the form of an attitudinal viewpoint from which he will experience and respond. The eighth Sephira indicates the ability to abstract, from experience, mental images, concepts, ideas, and thoughts based on the viewpoint or attitude (fourth Sephira) from which the experience is 'seen'. Ontological conceptualization or attitudes have a fixity or duration in time. Corporal Mind conceptualizations occur rapidly and form the almost constantly changing thought language of the conscious mind that we are all familiar with. Thoughts are not experiences of reality itself. They are abstractions of reality in the form of ideational symbols which represent reality.

The Corporal Energy Triad

The seventh and eighth Sephiroth also form the base of another triad which has its apex in the ninth Sephira (pointing down). This I will call the Corporal Energy Triad.

Shaddai El Chai is the name assigned to the ninth Sephira. It is translated as 'Omnipotent One'. El Chai is one of the compound names of God that Samuel Bousky decodes to mean Life Force (see Chapter Three). According to Sam, the Life Force is that which sustains all things including inanimate objects. In the Hindu philosophy it is called *prana* or *shakti* or *kundalini* (as it acts in the body). In the Chinese systems it is called *Ki*. In Theosophy and Anthroposophy it is called Ether (transpersonal) or etheric body (personal). In Western psychological thought it is called Libido (Freud), Psychic Energy (Jung), Orgone (Reich) and Bioenergy (Lowen).

As stated previously, energy is created by the duplication of Thot concerning the separation of locations in space within the space sphere. Energy at that stage fills the entire sphere of space. The additional Thot of mass acts to generate physical matter within the energy-filled space sphere. Almost mass-less matter, in the state we call energy, occupies the whole of space to this day. The ninth Sephira indicates the ability of a Quantum God to take in and utilize this ambient energy in his Body-Mind.

The seventh and eighth Sephira in the Corporal Energy Triad are the basic ways in which a Quantum God polarizes the energy of the ninth Sephira. The polarity is of positive and negative, *yin* and *yang*, male and female, all rolled into a basic dichotomy which is experienced subjectively through the Corporal Mind as thought and feeling. But the ninth Sephira is outside the mind and has no inherent polarity. The energy of the ninth Sephira is the stuff of which mentality and corporality are composed.

From the point of view of a Quantum God who is identified with his mind, he sees that he lives on various forms of energy which he gets from food and from the air. What he does not see from within his mind are the five Sephiroth which are outside the mind – the first three, the ninth and tenth. Since he is identified with his mind, anything which is outside it will not be conscious to him.

The ninth Sephira is on the Pillar of Being. It indicates the ability of a Quantum God to identify with energy. If he were occupying the state of being that this Sephira indicates then he would be outside the confines of his mind and be experiencing things in terms of their energetic effect on him and his energetic effect on the outside world and others. He would experience his thoughts and feelings as manifestations of energy transformations, and not simply as things which occur only in the mental realm.

The tenth Sephira bears the name Adonai Melekh. In the Qabalistic literature it is simply translated as 'God'. Adonai is a form of the title Lord. The root of his name indicates sovereignty or control over something. Melekh has roots in a word that has many meanings among which are: to pulverize, to rub with salt, to ingest salt, and a rag or old garment.

Salt is a typical and abundant form of solid, stable physical matter. This Sephira, located on the Pillar of Being, indicates the ability of a Quantum God to identify with, incorporate, and utilize physical matter (matter with a high degree of mass).

The Body Pattern Triad

The tenth Sephira is the apex of a large equilateral triangle (pointing down), formed by the seventh, eighth, and tenth Sephiroth. This large triangle includes the Corporal Energy Triad within it. I call it the Body Pattern Triad.

By drawing horizontal lines through the Sephiroth of the Body Pattern Triad we can distinguish three levels of functioning. The first level (the tenth Sephira) indicates the ability of a Quantum God to incorporate and structure the matter of the physcial universe into the form of a body.

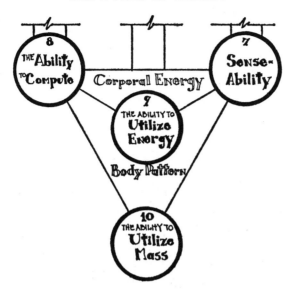

The next level includes the ninth Sephira and is concerned with the ability of a Quantum God to utilize the quality of energy which corresponds to the functional aspect of matter.

The third level of Body Pattern contains two Sephiroth. The seventh Sephira indicates the ability of a Quantum God to utilize energy in the form of feelings and emotions. The eighth Sephira is the ability of a Quantum God to utilize mass (patterning) in the form of concepts, ideas, and images. The seventh and eighth Sephiroth are really two aspects of the same mass-energy flow through the Body Pattern. Concepts act as structuring patterns for feelings. Feelings and sensations are the content of conceptualisation.

The Body Pattern is overlaid by the Corporal Energy Triad, which connects to the Corporal Mind through its common Sephiroth. The Corporal Mind is connected through the sixth Sephira to the Ontological Mind Triad. Thus the Tree of Life in the World of Ability sets the foundations for and is the pattern upon which the Worlds of Mind and Body are built.

8
The World of Mind

The Meaning of the Sephiroth and the Paths

The World of Mind is derived from Briah, the 'Archangelical World of Creations'. The Sephiroth in Briah bear the names of ten Archangels. Archangels are the personal messengers of God; also, His foremen. It is through the work of His Archangels that God creates, experiences, and controls His personal universe.

It is written that only God and Man are endowed with will, the ability to intend. Archangels and angels have no will of their own. They can only carry out the intent of a God. This suggests to me that Archangels and angels are personifications of aspects of a Quantum God and not individuals unto themselves.

In the model of Psychometaphysics, Archangels represent the ten basic modes of how a Quantum God creates, experiences, and controls his own personal reality, his subjective mind. These modes are the patterns (Briah corresponds to the second letter of Tetragrammaton, *hay*, the quality of pattern) through which a Quantum God structures his Thots.

The World of Ability describes ten basic categories of Thot. The World of Mind describes ten basic ways that a Quantum God structures his Thot. These structures become his subjective mentality. The World of Mind is a representation of an individual Quantum God's personal psychology. Psychology comes from the word *psyche* which means soul. The Quantum God is the spirit, his mind is his soul.

As the World of Ability suggests, all Quantum Gods have the same basic abilities. All Quantum Gods are functionally identical in nature. At the same time each Quantum God is unique in the ways he has chosen to use or pattern those abilities. These ways of functioning, although unique to each individual, fall into categories on a different level of activity, the mind.

To correlate the ten basic functioning patterns of the mind with the ten Sephiroth of the World of Mind, I have chosen to turn to the astrological symbols assigned to them in the World of Assiah. Assiah is the World of Matter. In the Psychometaphysical model, matter is a psychological function with respect to the nature of the Quantum Gods who produce it (by duplicating each other's Thots). I believe that the symbols of Assiah do not refer to matter itself but a subjective way of seeing matter. This is exactly what the World of Mind is concerned with. The World of Mind is concerned with the personal and subjective way a Quantum God chooses to perceive matter and others. His behavior is based on these perceptions and manifests in behavior patterns and reactions.

In using the symbols of Assiah to derive the meanings of the ten Sephiroth of Briah I am making these assumptions: firstly, that there is a direct connection in meaning between any Sephiroth in any of the four words and any other Sephira in the same location on its Tree of Life, i.e. the seventh Sephira in Briah is connected in meaning to the seventh Sephira in Atziluth, Yetzirah, and Assiah; secondly, I am assuming that whoever assigned the astrological symbols (which are at least as old as the symbolic Qabalah) to their Sephiroth was aware of the meaning of the Qabalistic system; and thirdly, that the symbols of Assiah have a meaning which can be derived simply from the contemplation of the symbols themselves without the need to refer to the vast amount of astrological commentaries concerning them.

The planetary symbols assigned to Assiah are primary symbols. The symbols yield the message of their meaning directly, within a specific context. The context is this: Each symbol indicates a specific pattern of functioning in the realm of the subjective mind.

The Planetary Symbols

All the planetary symbols of astrology are constructed of six basic components. They are as follows:

• The dot represents the Self or Quantum God in the prime state of consciousness. The dot, as has been pointed out, is the source of all graphic representation since all forms can be described as the loci of points or dots or as the activity of a dot. Here the dot represents pure being-ness.

O The circle indicates an expanded dot, representing the omni-directional activity or outer manifestation of being-ness. In the context of mentality it represents an individual Quantum God's awareness.

(The crescent represents receptivity or transmission of energy or information.

/ The arrow indicates movement, creativity, aggressiveness, or response.

— The horizontal line is female and passive.

| The vertical line is masculine and active.

+ The cross unites male and female. It represents the resultant balance or fixity of their joint manifestation.

Each of the planetary symbols can now be interpreted according to how these components are utilized in constructing the symbols. They will be read in the context of psychological functioning.

 The symbol for the Zodiac, as has been stated before, represents a relationship between Quantum Gods.

♄ The symbol for the planet Saturn. The Self is fixed (cross) above the crescent. In this case the crescent is attached to the male, active vertical line indicating a transmission of energy or information under the control of the Self. The Self, located above the crescent indicates that it has dominion over it. The absence of a circle indicates that this is a subconscious process (the circle indicates awareness). The symbol is a perfect representation of the process of Thot emanation which is normally unconscious to the mind. It indicates the idea of doing and creating in Thot.

♃ The symbol of the planet Jupiter. The crescent is attached to the female, passive line indicating receptivity from the same plane (horizontal receptivity suggests that it is concerned with communication of energy or information between one Quantum God and another). Again, there is no circle indicating a subconscious process. The Self is fixed (cross) in a certain attitudinal viewpoint from which it receives information from others. Psychologically, it is a good representation of a fixed attitude.

♂ The symbol of the planet Mars. It indicates awareness expressed or activity based on awareness. It represents the ability to respond or Response-Ability.

☉ The symbol for the sun. The dot (Self) within the circle (awareness) indicates an unfixed (no cross this time) state of being aware. It also depicts the Self dwelling in its own manifestation as a Quantum God dwells within the structure of his mind.

☿ The symbol of the planet Mercury. Receptivity (crescent) from above passes through awareness (circle) into fixity (cross) below. The symbol shows the process of perception, cognition, and retention. It represents quite clearly the process of conceptualization.

♀ The symbol of the planet Venus. Similar to Mercury, this symbol is missing the receptive crescent above it. It indicates awareness arising from an internal source, from within the body-mind and being fixed in conceptualization below. It is a good representation of the cognition of sensations and feelings which are perceived from within the body-mind.

The symbol for the Moon. It represents unconceptualized and unconditioned transmission or reception of energy or information, below mental awareness. The Moon reflects the Sun and so I take it to indicate a state of energy, just as the Sun indicates a state of being.

The symbol of the Earth. The cross within the circle hides the dot at its center. It represents the Self identified with (fixed within) the body-mind awareness. It is a good representation of the character structure or personality.

These are the planetary symbols which are assigned to the ten Sephiroth of Assiah. We can now place the key ideas for each of the symbols in their designated positions on the Tree of Life in the World of Mind.

As the reader may notice, the second and third Sephiroth are the reverse of how they are shown in the World of Ability. This is because we are now correlating the Sephiroth with their astrological symbols in Assiah, and not with the names of God as was done in the World of Ability. (See Chapter Three.)

Since, in the World of Mind, we are dealing with the quality of Pattern, it is appropriate here to describe the Paths which connect the Sephiroth since they form the pattern on which the Sephiroth hang. Each of the twenty-two Paths is assigned an astrological symbol. Ten of the Paths bear planetary symbols (Neptune, Uranus, and Pluto replace the dot, Zodiac, and the Earth) and the twelve signs of the Zodiac are assigned to the remaining twelve Paths.

The symbols of the signs are not primary symbols as are the planetary ones. They refer to a vast body of mythology and commentaries concerning their meanings. To simplify things, I have

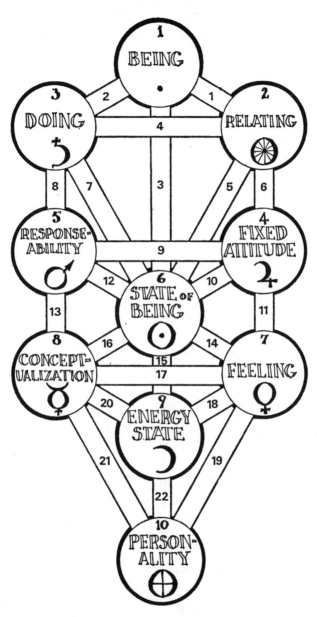

THE WORLD OF MIND

chosen to use the key ideas assigned to the signs by C. C. Zain in his *Sacred Tarot*.[18] They are as follows:

ARIES	I AM
TAURUS	I HAVE
GEMINI	I THINK
CANCER	I FEEL
LEO	I WILL
VIRGO	I ANALYZE
LIBRA	I BALANCE
SCORPIO	I DESIRE
SAGGITARIUS	I SEE
CAPRICORN	I USE
AQUARIUS	I KNOW
PISCES	I BELIEVE

Each Path will be interpreted primarily on the basis of the two Sephiroth it connects and the meaning of the astrological symbols assigned to them. The Hebrew letters,[4] the Tarot cards[4] and other corresponding ideas connected to the meaning of the Paths, will be utilized as secondary clues to their meanings. In addition we have their meanings as described in the World of Ability, the English translations of the Archangelical names of Briah,[2] the English translations of the titles of the Sephiroth,[2] and the appellations assigned to the Sephiroth by the Sephir Yetzirath.[2]

The Supernal Triad

As in the World of Ability, the Supernals are the source of the seven remaining Sephiroth. Since they are above the Abyss, they are not actually contained within the mind. The Superiors function through the Inferiors and are reflected by them. The Supernals will be described as they are 'seen' from within the mind (represented by the Inferiors).

The World of Ability is a description of the nature of a Quantum God from the point of view of the first Sephira, Being. The World of Mind is a description of the nature of a Quantum God from the point of view of the sixth Sephira. The sixth Sephira occupies the second position down on the Pillar of Being.

This position corresponds to the second letter of the Tetragrammaton, indicating the aspect of Pattern. This is consistent with the meaning of the World of Mind. The first Sephira of the Inferiors is the fourth, Fixed Attitudes. The Superiors will therefore be described in the World of Mind as they relate to fixed attitudes.

The First Sephira: Being

Title of all No. 1 Sephiroth	Kether, Crown
Yetziratic appellation	Hidden Intelligence
Archangel	Metatron, The Angel of the Presence
Symbol in Assiah	Point or Vortex

As the Archangelic name implies, this Sephira is the representative of the Being of a Quantum God in the realm of the mind. The presence of the Self, as viewed and experienced from within the mind is not the Self at all, but its mental equivalent – an attitude or belief concerning the Self. The mind is constructed on mental images, which represent real things, but which act to block their direct apprehension. Any mental image arising from a viewpoint toward the Self hinders the individual from experiencing the Self directly.

Any attitude or belief about the Self, no matter how accurate it may be, is simply a reflection of how we have chosen to see the Self from within the Mind. The mind, by its very nature, is incapable of creating an image which can replace the Self or accurately represent it. The Self exists beyond all viewpoints, attitudes, beliefs, and their attendant images. As will be pointed out in Part Three, one must dis-identify from all mentality in order to experience directly (gain enlightenment of) one's Self.

Some of the more common beliefs concerning the Self are exemplified by the currently accepted religious and scientific philosophies, which have been internalized in the mental attitudes of individuals. While psychologists and psychiatrists minimize to varying degrees the importance of religious beliefs in the personality of the individual, they are the foundation attitudes upon which the other attitudes of the mind are based. Religious beliefs include any beliefs to which the individual assigns first cause or which are his personal cosmological model or program. In this sense, scientific and atheistic belief systems are also religious in nature.

The common interpretations of the religious cosmologies of Judaism, Christianity, Hinduism, Buddhism, Islam, Taoism, and many others, have one basic belief in common. This belief implies that the individual does not actually exist independently but is seen as the creation of an omnipotent power called God, by many different names. The belief in a solitary God who creates the universe and all the individuals within it has some interesting consequences.

Firstly, it implies that each of us is not the source of what we do or what happens to us in the world and gives rise to the belief in fate or 'God's Will'. This attitude resigns a human being to the manipulations of others and takes away much of his incentive to improve his lot in life. Parallel with this is the usually unconscious belief that one is, in the deepest sense, not responsible for one's acts. God is responsible. An individual with this attitude can never really be responsible for himself, although he may act responsibly in the socially accepted manner.

Secondly, a person who subscribes to the one God belief will never experience his life as having an ultimate purpose. Why would a single God create the universe? Is life not a game He is playing with Himself? What is the purpose of it all? Since a unitary God implies a purposeless universe, the attitude that an individual is incapable of understanding life's purpose is also assumed in order to relieve the individual of the responsibility of having to look for himself. With the attitude that he cannot know, it will never occur to him to question his beliefs.

Thirdly, it implies that there is no real Self or Quantum God. With this attitude, even when a person goes to the depths of direct experience in some form of enlightenment process and experiences himself as he is in Negative Existence, alone and formless, he will be unable to conceive of his true nature as a Quantum God. He will, when he looks back on his experience mentally, proclaim his oneness with God and the universe but deny that he is God. A believer in the one God cannot even conceive of the reality of separate, individual Gods of which he is one. The thought would never occur to him. This is why enlightenment must be accompanied by the clearing of the mind of all fixed attitudes. This is why some people who have had spontaneous enlightenment experiences end up in mental institutions or must hide themselves away from others in monasteries or convents. In order to integrate the enlightenment experience into the mental framework of everyday life, the mind must be as flexible and unfixed as possible. Mental attitudes should be based on direct experience, rather than attempting to fit direct experience into the existing fixed attitudes and beliefs of the mind.

One of the currently accepted beliefs about the Self is that it is simply a product of the survival of the fittest, a complex stimulus-response mechanism, or a mental construct resulting from social influences. These beliefs imply that all the spiritually-oriented beliefs are simply mental contructs and that there is no essential Self aside from the animal nature of the body. A person who subscribes to these belief systems will not find it easy to conceive of there being anything else, since his beliefs block the experience of other possibilities. He will instead ascribe all 'spiritual' aspects of himself and others to the functioning of the brain (or mis-functioning, as the case may be).

A belief or attitudinal viewpoint about the Self is a mental program which hides the fact of the existence of the programmer. Once a person has programmed himself into his computer (by identifying with a belief system) he is lost to his own direct experience.

The Second Sephira: Relating

Title of all No. 2 Sephiroth	Chokmah, Wisdom
Yetziratic appellation	Illuminating Intelligence
Archangel	Raziel, Herald of Deity
Symbol in Assiah	The Zodiac

The symbol of the Zodiac represents a relationship between Gods. I believe that it is consistent with the meaning of the God name Jehovah Elohim assigned to the third Sephira in Atziluth.

A Quantum God depends on the existence of others for his own existence. Without the existence of others there would be no individuality, no consciousness (defined in Psychometaphysics as the primary state arising as a result of a communication in Thot with others), and no creation (it is actually a co-creation). This is as much a fact of everyday human existence as it is a metaphysical axiom.

Mental attitudes and beliefs about others and one's relationship to others take the place of the experience of the above fact in the mind. An individual who does not want to experience his basic dependence on others will erect attitudes which give him a mental framework in which to experience himself as being totally independent. The basic belief upon which such attitudes are built is the belief in the one outside God. Mentally this implies that: a) there are no others (they are all pieces of God); b) that others are simply ideas or objects of the mind and are therefore controllable, as are thoughts; and c) that relationships come after work, duty to one's beliefs, religion, and patriotism, in that order of importance.

The belief that others are stimulus-response mechanisms or social constructs has similar ramifications in the mind. Life's purpose, with respect to these beliefs will seem to be survival, competition, and the gaining of power over others, rather than contacting the God within others.

The Third Sephira: Doing

Title of all No. 3 Sephiroth	Binah, Understanding
Yetziratic Appellation	Sanctifying Intelligence
Archangel	Tsaphiel, Contemplation of God
Symbol in Assiah	Saturn

Again, if we were to switch the symbols of the second and third Sephiroth they would make more sense; Wisdom (the second Sephira), which is a quality an individual has, fits nicely with the idea of an individual doer (symbolized by Saturn), while Understanding (the third Sephira), which is what takes place between two or more individuals, fits the idea of relationship (symbolized by the Zodiac).

While a Quantum God is dependent for his existence on the presence of others, he is, nevertheless, totally responsible for all that he creates for himself and others. A Quantum God does nothing except by his intent, for it is his intentionality (Thot) which is his means of doing. This is true in everyday human affairs as well. Although we all have attitudes and beliefs which limit our consciousness of how much we are responsible for what we do to ourselves, others, and what 'happens' to us, on a very basic level we are each totally responsible.

The level at which we are each totally responsible for our acts is at the level of the Self. This level is usually subconscious to the mind since we all have beliefs about who or what causes things and whether or not they are intentional acts. The extreme attitudes are: a) that God, society, or fate is the final cause, in which case no one is really responsible for intending it to happen; and b) that one is totally responsible, and therefore must bear the burden of, and be punished for, one's acts. Even if one accepts the premise that one is totally responsible for the way one is in the world, because one is identified with the mind and not with the Self, one is helpless to change the way things are.

A person with some degree of self-enlightenment knows that he is the doer. He creates his mental programs, his personal façades, and may, if he goes deep enough, realize that he also creates what appears just to 'happen' to him. But, if he makes this fact an attitude in his mind, he may begin to believe that he alone is responsible. The universe is a co-creation and every event that happens in it is a result of the intentionality of all those involved in it. Without the accompanying life enlightenment which is the experience of this fact, an individual may take the attitude that he is God, the only God. This attitude produces the behavior we categorize under the heading of megalomania, the belief that there is one doer and the person in question is it. The direct experience of another immediately gets rid of any idea that Godliness is exclusive to oneself.

In the case of fate or accident, the individuals involved are individually responsible for the doing of it and participating in it. There is no dictator or government in the world which can make anyone, who is in contact with his essential Self, do anything. It is our belief system alone which allows us to give up the responsibility for being the intentional doer, and, at the same time, give our power away to others or fate. It is our basic intentionality which is the cause and not our mental programs about it. There are no accidents. There is no fate. These are mental attitudes which allow us to escape temporarily from the fact that we are, on a very deep level, getting out of life exactly what we want.

Path No. 1, Self and Other

The first Path connects the Sephira of Being (first Sephira) with the Sephira of Relating (second Sephira). It is assigned the letter *aleph,* corresponds to the first Tarot card, the Fool (numerically zero), and the planet Uranus.

The symbol for Uranus indicates a communication taking place above awareness. The communication is one of Thot emanation between two or more Quantum Gods.

Aleph has no sound of its own in Hebrew but is an exhalation of breath and indicates the word of God as it is referred to in scripture. Again, it is a good representation of Thot emanation, the essential creative activity of a Quantum God.

The Fool card suggests to me the mystery of the existence of the Self. Although the Self exists with respect to others, it is not knowable to others except by what it does in relationship with others. If the Self or Quantum God were to cease emanating his Thots, he would not exist with respect to anyone else. So, the Self both exists and doesn't exist, depending on how we choose to think of it. Conceptually, there is no way of having these opposite viewpoints at the same time.

All mental attitudes are based on an aspect of the truth. But, since they are viewpoints and not direct experiences, they distort the truth at the same time. The mental attitudes which give the impression that the Self is a product of the social context we live in are true in their way. And the attitude that the Self exists apart from its relationship with others is also true in its relative way. Yet both of these attitudes contradict each other, while the truth itself has no dichotomy.

Path No. 2, All Doing is Intentional

The second Path connects the Sephira of Being (first Sephira) with the Sephira of Doing (third Sephira). It bears the letter *bayt,* corresponds to the second Tarot card, the Magician (numerically one), and the planet Mercury.

The symbol for Mercury indicates the process of conceptualization. On this level, however, it represents the basis of conceptualization which is Thot emanation. Thot, again, is a quantum of specific intentionality. A Quantum God 'conceptualizes' the things around him by having the Thot that they exist. We have no word in English which means this except for the idea of creation. The closest mental equivalent is the idea of conceptualization.

It is through Thot emanation that a Quantum God does things or creates things. With respect to the mind the things that he does in Thot seems to manifest magically. Thoughts and feelings appear magically out of nowhere and things happen to people without them being mentally aware that they have intended them to happen. The Magician card in the Tarot represents these apparently magical occurrences. The Magician has a table in front of him. On the table are four tools which he uses to perform his 'magic'. They are the scepter or wand, a cup, a coin or pentacle, and a sword or knife. These represent the four aspects of the Tetragrammaton (Force, Pattern, Activity, and Form). It is a picture of the Self and its basic abilities in the realm of Thot or intentionality. All that the magician does, he does with his intentionality.

Path No. 4, The Energy of Relating

The fourth Path connects the Sephira of Relating (second Sephira) with the Sephira of Doing (third Sephira). It is assigned the letter *dallet,* corresponds to the Empress card in the Tarot, and the planet Venus.

The symbol for Venus indicates an awareness arising from within oneself. On this level it indicates the influence of Thot communication with others as it affects the individual. In the body-mind these exchanges will manifest as feelings and emotions.

The Empress in the Tarot also represents the inner power or influence that we have on others and they on us. Again, in the body-mind, it manifests as emotional power, exemplified by the woman behind the throne, an archetype who represents the unseen power of relationship.

The corresponding attitudes in the mind range between these two extremes – dependence and independence. The attitude that one is independent of others can give one the sense of being invulnerable, while the attitude that one is dependent gives a sense of vulnerability. Both are true, or neither are true.

As will be pointed out in the chapter on enlightenment, one of the most popular methods of gaining self-enlightenment is isolating oneself from all others and their influence. This is moving on the fourth Path in the direction of individual aloneness. It is a withdrawal from life and relationship with others. In the state of aloneness, one can get in touch with the creative ability that one is, and experience the limitless possibilities and capabilities of the Self alone. In the other direction, however, one finds, as one approaches and re-enters life and relationship with others, that the creative capacity of the individual is limited by the creative capacity of all others. Alone one is God. In relationship to others, one is simply human.

The Paths Crossing the Abyss

The fourth Path completes the Supernal Triad. The Supernals, as has been pointed out, are not actually a part of the Inferior seven. The Inferiors are reflections and manifestations of the Supernals. There is no mentality within the Superiors, i.e. they are not contained within the mind itself. The description of them so far has only been in the terms of mental attitudes towards the Superiors, and not the nature of the Superiors themselves.

The transition from the Superiors into the Inferiors is made by crossing over the Abyss. The Abyss in the World of Mind is the barrier between the process of Thot emanation and duplication and the way that an individual Quantum God chooses to experience the Thot reality in his own subjective manner. There are five Paths which connect the Superiors to the Inferiors and therefore cross the Abyss: Paths No. 3, 5, 6, 7, and 8. They represent the five basic attitudes upon which all mental attitudes, beliefs, and assumptions are based. These attitudes mirror the conditions placed on matter by the Quantum Gods (see Chapter Seven) when they created matter.

These attitudes upon which the mind is constructed do not concern matter. They are Thots about the Quantum God and his Thot. They therefore condition his being-ness just as the Thots about matter condition matter. The attitudes are: Mental Being-ness, Ontological Time, Ontological Space, Ontological Energy, and Ontological Mass. The ramifications of these five subjective attitudes create the mind as we know it.

Path No. 3, Mental Being-ness

The third Path connects Being (first Sephira) to State of Being (sixth Sephira). It is assigned the letter *gimel*, the High Priestess card in the Tarot, and the Moon.

This Path indicates the incarnation of the Quantum God (essential Self) into the central position within the mind as represented by the sixth Sephira. To do this the Quantum God must identify with his mind (have the Thot that the mind is what he is). The symbol of the Moon, in the receptive sense, indicates the process of identification with something, in this case the mind. The beingness of the Self is received into the mind. In the active sense, the Quantum God is placing himself in control of, and under the direct influence of, his mental functioning.

This Path represents the connection between a Quantum God's normal waking mental consciousness and his Self, which is at once within the mind in the form of attitudes about the Self and, at the same time, remains outside of the mind since the mind cannot completely contain the Self.

The High Priestess is pictured sitting on a throne within the Inferiors of the Tree of Life (symbolized by the two pillars in the background or some tree-like form). Her position indicates that she is within the Tree and now looks at the observer from that viewpoint. She is at once showing us that we are viewing the world from our own mental construct, our own Tree of Life, and at the same time pointing out that she is not merely a part of the Tree but an individual occupying it. The card represents the inner knowing that occurs when an individual contacts the real Self among the artefacts of the mind. Suddenly things which are impossible to perceive through the mind are perceived from the essential Self. The Self knows all there is to know, since it created all things. But this fundamental ability to know all things is hidden by the mind which has, as its main function, the hiding of things which the individual wishes to keep unconscious.

Path No. 5, Ontological Time

Path five connects the Sephira of Relating (second Sephira) to State of Being (sixth Sephira). It bears the letter *hay* and corresponds to the Emperor in the Tarot. The sign of Aries is placed here, indicating the key idea 'I am'.

Ontological time is the attitude or basic belief that a Quantum God exists continuously. This attitude helps to identify the Quantum God with those processes which do occur in time such as the body-mind process. Essentially a Quantum God, and his Thots, do not occur in time. Since he sees reality through this attitude, he will be unaware of his Thot emanations which are the activities of his essential Self outside of time. He will, instead, only be aware of his thoughts and feelings which occur in time, which are the manifestations of his now subconscious intentionalities (Thots).

This Path indicates the effect of Relating on the State of Being. The attitude 'I am' in the mind takes a form of dependence on others for one's self-esteem. In all societies, to one degree or another, children are dependent on their parents and the social reality for the values which connect to their sense of self within their society. Most of us spend a lot of energy trying to please others in such a way that we can imagine that they hold us in esteem or have respect or love for us.

Since the mind is a way of controlling our subjective reality, it is important for someone who is identified with his mind to control what other people think of him as well. Subjective reality can only appear to be objective when others agree with it in their own minds. This is the mental-social counterpart of the co-created reality that occurs in the Supernal realm of Thot duplication.

Our parents and our society set the rules for taking on the socially accepted attitudes concerning our relationship with others. We are taught from an early age to produce a façade with which to face the world. The façade is based on the values of society. We value politeness, predictability, niceness, obedience, collecting data instead of direct experience, patriotism, institutional religion as a ceremony, and the current trends in attitudes passed on through education. These attitudes lead to social success. All this is based on the attitude that left to his own unfettered, natural inclinations, a human being is dangerous. Charles Berner's definition for ego is 'the mental image you have of yourself which is based on what you think others think of you'.

Path No. 6, Ontological Space

Path six connects Relating (second Sephira) with Fixed Attitudes (fourth Sephira). It bears the symbol for Taurus whose key idea is 'I have'. The letter is *vav,* the Tarot correspondent is the Hierophant.

Ontological space is an attitude or belief that a Quantum God is located in space. This attitude acts in combination with the attitude that he exists in time to produce a mental framework in which a Quantum God further ties himself to the perceptions and reactions of his mind. He then perceives himself as being located in a different position in space with respect to other Quantum Gods. While all Quantum Gods essentially occupy the whole of space, he now experiences himself tied to one location in space, a point of consciousness within his body-mind.

The Hierophant is the Egyptian equivalent to the pope or head priest. He represents the spiritual law-giver, the one who decides what is to be believed in and what is not. The religious leader is the final source of how to interpret natural or God's law and live by it. The laws thus interpreted determine the moral code of all individuals who subscribe to that religion.

The equivalent to the outside religious dogma of a church, within the individual, is the accumulated fixed attitudes indicated by the fourth Sephira. Whatever code of ethics, morality, or religious dogma that a person subscribes to, whether they were born into it or chose at some point to believe in them, is introjected into the mind in the form of fixed attitudes and beliefs. In most cases a person is born into religion and is subject to the existing religious or ethical beliefs of others, his parents, teachers, ministers, priests, and hierophants. These beliefs then become the foundations upon which the individual will judge reality and react to it.

Path No. 7, Ontological Mass

The seventh Path connects Doing (third Sephira) with State of Being (sixth Sephira). It bears the letter *zayn*, the Lovers card in the Tarot, and the sign of Gemini, 'I think'.

This Path is the transition from the realm of direct action and experience through the process of Thot emanation to the process of thinking – an indirect, mental equivalent of Thot emanation. In the Supernals, each Thot is a specific intentionality existing outside of time and is completely separate and unconnected to any other Thot which may have occurred before or after its emanation. There is no cause and effect relationship between one Thot and another. A Quantum God simply has one Thot and then has another. The Thot that Thots are connected to each other in time and space is an additional Thot which gives rise to the mental thinking process. The Thot that Thots occur in a sequence is the ontological equivalent in the mind of the Thot that the locations that a matter$_1$ quantum occupies occur in a sequence. In the material world this Thot gives rise to the quality of mass. In the mental world this Thot gives rise to mental structures such as concepts, ideas, and images. Thoughts occur in a sequence of time and are connected together by their similarity of meaning or consequence.

This Path also indicates an identification by a Quantum God with the structural qualities of his body-mind. The structural or patterning aspect is the mental functioning itself. And so a Quantum God identifies himself with his mind through the Path of Ontological Mass.

When this attitude is contacted in the enlightenment process, a person may say that he is his mind or that he is a thought he is having. Many of us in the Western world place value on our thinking process and are identified with it.

Path No. 8, Ontological Energy

The eighth Path connects Doing (third Sephira) to Response Ability (fifth Sephira). It bears the letter *chayt*, the Chariot card in the Tarot, and the sign of Cancer, 'I feel'.

Thot (intentionality) is the source of both thought and feeling. Thought is the mass component of Thot and manifests in the body-mind as mental images and electrical brain functions Feeling is the energy component of Thot and manifests in the body as energy transactions throughout the tissues of the body and the nervous system as a whole.

This Path indicates an identification with the energy aspects of the body-mind. The identification results in a dependency on sensations, feelings, and emotions as the primary means of perception. Through this Path a Quantum God identifies himself with his body and sees the world through his body-consciousness.

Energy is one of the last things from which a person going through an enlightenment process will dis-identify himself. When this attitude is contacted the individual may proclaim that 'I am energy', or some variation such as consciousness-as-energy or light. Quite often this stage of the enlightenment process is mistaken as the final one since it is difficult for the mind to conceive of anything more 'spiritual' than energy. But a Quantum God is not energy; he is the source of all energy.

The Ontological Mind Triad

The five paths which cross the Abyss connect the Supernal Triad to the next triad below them, the Ontological Mind Triad. These five paths act together to bring the Quantum God into incarnation, into the body-mind, the process of identifying himself with his mental and physical functioning. The attitudes of Ontological time, space, energy, and mass condition the being-ness of the Quantum God so that he can locate himself within the body and function through it. Without these imposed conditions on his being-ness he would be like a disembodied spirit. These are the paths leading the infinite being-ness of a Quantum God into the realm of the human being.

The World of Mind stands between the World of Ability and

the World of Body. This indicates that the mind is closer to the Quantum God than his body. This is exemplified by the average human being who finds his subjective mentality to be more directly accessible to him than his body. The body, once cleared of fixed mental attitudes, tells us what is actually going on in the objective reality. The mind, as we are describing it here, stands as a filter between the Self and the body. It functions to distort the perceptions and sensations of the body in such a way as to produce an entirely subjective view of reality. This is the function of the fourth Sephira, the first Sephira of the Ontological Mind Triad.

Since I am using the word mind in a unique sense, I want to clarify what I mean by it. Most of us think of intelligence when we think of mentality. But intelligence, in this model, is an attribute of the essential Self (Quantum God). Mentality is simply the subjective patterns into which otherwise naturally flowing thoughts are structured. Mentality is a result of an attempt to control one's perceptions, rather than allowing the bodily functions free rein to produce their own picture of reality.

The Fourth Sephira: Fixed Attitudes

Title of all No. 4 Sephiroth	Chesed, Mercy
Yetziratic Appellation	Recepticular or Cohesive Intelligence
Archangel	Tsadkiel, The Justice of God
Symbol in Assiah	Jupiter

Mercy is an exemption from the natural or expected consequences of one's acts. In the mind, attitudes and beliefs function in the same way to exempt from awareness those acts which the individual believes himself not to be responsible for, and those things which he is unwilling to experience consciously.

The Archangelic name which indicates justice implies that there must be some body of law, either natural or contrived, by which justice is meted out. In the individual, the body of moral law by which he judges things is his set of mental fixed attitudes and beliefs.

With reference to the Yetziratic Appellation, which is translated as Recepticular or Cohesive Intelligence, the functions of the

Ontological Mind fit perfectly. As we shall see in the following discussion of the fourth Sephira, the subjective mind is concerned with the way objective reality (as perceived through the bodily senses) is received by the individual (recepticular) and the way he connects one perception to another (cohesive).

In the World of Ability, this Sephira indicates the ability of a Quantum God to take an attitudinal viewpoint. Here, in the World of Mind, that ability manifests in the establishment of fixed attitudes, beliefs, and primary assumptions. A fixed attitude gives rise to mental images. These mental images act as filters or lenses through which the experience of the body, and hence the physical world and others, is viewed. After an attitude has been taken by the individual toward some aspect of life, the mental images connected to that attitude will block all sensory data which do not conform to those images. A person who believes, i.e. takes the attitude that, life is full of stumbling-blocks will experience his life in just that way. Those aspects of life which are without stumbling-blocks will not enter his awareness since they do not fit his preconceived image of how life is.

Fixed attitudes also block an individual's experience of himself beyond his body. The assumption or belief that one is no more than a body or mind blocks all communication between the mental-physical aspects of the person and his transcendental or transpersonal nature as a Quantum God. Whatever images he has of himself will keep the direct experience of his true nature out of reach of his awareness.

A fixed attitude is normally unconscious to the person viewing things through it. Just as we are usually unaware of our eyes as we look at something we are unaware of the attitudinal lens which colors that which is perceived through it.

But all subconscious fixed attitudes were, at some time, conscious. They are the remnants of conscious, intentional decisions that we have made concerning how we have decided to see things. For example, the patient of a therapist complained of impotence and a basic discomfort with people of the opposite sex. In a session of Gestalt therapy, using hypnosis, the patient was able to remember an incident in his childhood. His mother had punished him for something he had done and, in that moment of emotional turmoil, he decided never again to trust a woman or put himself in the position of being at the mercy of a woman. Almost forty years after the decision was made the attitude of distrust toward women still had a tremendous influence in his life. And yet all this time passed without him being conscious of the attitude he had taken quite consciously in his childhood. This particular attitude had a tremendous effect on his physiological functioning so that, even though he consciously wanted to have a satisfying relationship, he was unable to respond.

The function of an attitude is to inhibit sensory awareness. In the example above, the man did not want to experience his dependence on his mother. And so he took an attitude which would give him the subjective feeling that he was not dependent on her or subject to her judgements and punishments. The fact is that he was dependent. The attitude was taken to change the reality of the situation into one which was less threatening to his survival and mental well-being.

Most of our basic attitudes come from our parents. Yet it is the individual who accepts them or rejects them. It is the individual who determines which attitude he will take in any given circumstance. It is the individual who does it, and who must take responsibility for having done it, if any change it is to occur.

The attitude is created by the Quantum God through the use of his Thot. This is why babies who have yet to talk are able to take attitudes just as an adult can do. A fixed attitude is not just a product of the adult conceptual mind. It is a condition of being which affects the whole character structure and the functioning of the body.

When the mind is set into a fixed attitude, it collects all the energy of the experience that is being had from that attitude into images. The images bind the energy of that which the person is unwilling to experience so that they do not come into that person's awareness. Until the image is contacted, and the energy that it contains is experienced, it will remain in the mind. In the mind these images act as barriers which limit the capacity of an individual to respond to and experience that which lies behind the attitudes he has taken.

The Fifth Sephira: Response-Ability

Title of all No. 5 Sephiroth	Geburah, Severity
Yetziratic Appellation	Radical Intelligence
Archangel	Samiel, The Severity of God
Symbol in Assiah	Mars

The fifth Sephira emerges out of the fourth. The ability to respond, the capacity of an individual to act with awareness is determined by the quality and quantity of fixed attitudes and beliefs he holds. Fixed attitudes act to deaden the sensory awareness of the individual and restrict his ability to respond on many levels. By respond, I mean to include mental and emotional response as well as physical response.

One aspect of intelligence is the ability to differentiate between things. A person with an attitude which tends to obscure the differences between people will tend to respond to people as if they were all the same. His ability to respond to the differences between people is restricted by his attitude.

A person who holds attitudes concerning the 'proper' behavior of people in certain situations or what words should be used in polite conversation will respond automatically when someone acts other than how he believes they should. Swear words evoke strong emotional responses in people who have these kinds of attitudes.

Most of us have attitudes concerning our emotional responses and how and where they should be expressed. For example, a person that has an attitude that anger is never appropriate will tend to hold it back on every occasion that it arises. The attitude will result in a chronic set of tensions in the body as the body holds the anger back. The energy of the suppressed anger may even affect his health or do damage to an organ of his body. The overall effect will be a chronic tension which he is unable to relax. A situation will occur in which the person gets angry. The situation may be something quite insignificant in itself but it will overwhelm the ability of the person to hold back all the stored anger in his body from the countless times when anger was suppressed. The dam will burst and he may fly into a rage, losing control of himself. He will then experience his anger as being irrational or ungentlemanly, as indeed it is. The response caused by the sudden flood of emotion will reinforce his attitude that anger should never be expressed and the vicious cycle of attitude-response will be reinforced. A common, associated attitude with this syndrome is the belief that anger is always expressed irrationally and leads to violence. But anger is a natural response of the body to certain situations. Without the restrictive attitudes it is always appropriate to the situation and does not lead to violence. It becomes irrational and violent because of the restrictions placed on it. But most of us are afraid to experience our own anger and the anger of another and so we institute generally accepted attitudes about it which our parents and teachers reinforce.

We all have our favorite ways of responding to our own emotions and the emotions of others. These are the results of our mental programs, the set of attitudes which lie below awareness and condition our responses to life and others.

The body, free of fixed attitudes, has an innate wisdom. It knows exactly how much water and food it needs, how best to breathe and function under almost all circumstances. Mental attitudes get in the way of the otherwise natural functioning of the body, constricting the breathing, causing excessive eating and drinking of the wrong things. Attitudes turn an otherwise naturally graceful and limber body into a rigid and awkward object, continually in need of control.

Path No. 9, The Split of Intentionality

The ninth Path connects Fixed Attitudes (fourth Sephira) to Response-Ability (fifth Sephira). It is assigned the letter *tayt*, and the Tarot card called Strength. The sign of Leo which has the key idea of 'I will' is placed here.

As has been pointed out, the Ability to Respond is directly proportional to the amount of fixed attitudes that exist in the mind. Will is a key word here because pre-mental intentionality (Thot) is split into two opposing functions of mental will. In the creation of fixed attitudes, a Quantum God is willing through thought the way he wants to experience (by eliminating all other possible viewpoints from consciousness). On the other hand, he is willing responses or actions based on his perceptions through his fixed attitudes. Intention is split between response and restrictions on response. This basic split of intentionality into will and anti-will is manifested throughout the mind and becomes a way of life for the Quantum God who has identified with his mentality.

The split of the will is the basic plague of the mind. A person is told and believes that learning something is difficult. He creates an attitude which says that he cannot learn such things. Then and thereafter he will find it a difficult effort of the will when he attempts to learn. Every basic ability lies dormant as a potential capacity within each individual. All these capacities are restricted in one way or another by the attitudes of the mind.

The split will is responsbile for the inability to express and take in (feel) the emotions that are stuck within fixed attitudes about the expression of certain emotions. Therapy in this area requires a search into the intentionality behind both the attitude and its manifestation as an emotional 'stuckness' or block. In almost every case, the energy of the emotions is released and becomes available when the corresponding attitude is changed. This requires that the person is willing to experience and express the emotion bound within the attitude and remember the circumstance under which the attitude was taken on. He must then make a conscious decision to drop the attitude or replace it with one that allows the emotion.

Much that comes under the heading of self-improvement also comes under the heading of removing the fixed attitudes which block the creative capability of the individual.

This ninth Path hides, behind it, the creative capability described in the chapter entitled The Creative Law. Acting from one's Self, the act of creation in all realms is a simple, natural function. In the split-intentionality of mental will, life becomes an effort. It requires that a Quantum God fight his own counterintentionality, which is now a part of his character structure.

Path No. 10, Retreating from Experience

The tenth Path connects Fixed Attitudes (fourth Sephira) to

State of Being (sixth Sephira). It corresponds to the letter *yod*, the Hermit in the Tarot, and the sign of Virgo. The key idea behind Virgo is 'I analyze'.

Fixed attitudes are the means by which a Quantum God analyzes reality. Each fixed attitude separates him from his direct experience of life and gives him a relatively removed place from which to experience reality. This conditions his very being into the adult-like intellectual experiencer, who would rather experience his thoughts about things and others than things and others themselves.

This function of stepping back from direct experience allows him to have control over how he is affected by his environment. At the same time it places him in the position of the hermit by isolating his essential Self from the direct experience of life and others. From this position, however, he sees himself as objective and wise. This attitude is supported by the socially constructed reality in which objectivity is valued and direct experience is mistrusted. The wisdom which is represented by the Hermit comes from choosing more inclusive attitudes, i.e. ones that take a greater part of reality into account. The wisdom is, however, only mental. The greatest sages in history are not known for their ability to respond to life and others but rather their attractive way of looking at things.

Path No. 12, Helpless Is As Helpless Does

The twelfth Path connects Response-Ability (fifth Sephira) to State of Being (sixth Sephira). It bears the letter *lammed*, the Justice card in the Tarot, and the sign of Libra, 'I balance'.

Response-Ability has two sides to it. The ability to respond is directly proportional to how much responsibility one takes for being able. The balance is one of self-determination versus environmental circumstance as the determining factor. It is the balance between personal maturity (self-reliance) and immaturity (relying excessively on others or circumstance). The balance between these determines the state of being that one is in.

The more attitudes you have which deny your responsibility, the more you find that you are unable to effect a change in your circumstances. The lack of ability is the justice for the attitude or state of being in which you experience yourself as being not responsible. For example, if there is something about yourself you do not like, you must first take responsibility for having made it that way. Only by accepting responsibility for it can you change it. The alternative is to blame others or to take the attitude that that is simply your nature and cannot be changed.

The Sixth Sephira: State of Being

Title of all No. 6 Sephiroth	Tiphareth, Beauty
Yetziratic Appellation	Mediating Intelligence
Archangel	Michael, Like Unto God
Symbol in Assiah	The Sun

A state of being is a role that an individual plays out in his interactions with others in life. The basic roles are those that we are all familiar with – child, parent, adult, good boy or good girl, top dog or underdog, good citizen, or radical revolutionary, and so on. These roles are the reflections of the effects of sets of fixed attitudes or beliefs which connect with each other and form personality structure. These personality structures have their attendant behavior patterns, manners of thinking, and emotional response patterns.

These roles change under the varying circumstances of life. Other roles overlay them, the roles and states of being which are established by one's vocation – doctor, soldier, diplomat, and so on. All these roles constellate around a central mental image with which the individual tends to identify himself. This is the ego.

The ego is a complex set of mental images which depict, in the subjective mind, an image of who a person is in the world. The image is based on one thing; one's relationship with others. The ego is the sum total of what you think others think of you. Behind it is its reflection, what you think of yourself. But the two are interdependent. For if your self-image is not believable to others it will not serve its purpose.

All these mental images, including the ego, circulate around the sixth Sephira. Since this is where the Quantum God is, he will experience life and others through the medium of these self-created images. In turn, he will act in accordance with these images in order to preserve them. He preserves them since they are his means of controlling his subjective reality and can sometimes aid him in controlling others. But, since he has identified himself with his images, he is out of contact with his true nature which lies behind them.

The fourth and fifth Sephiroth are on the pillars of Relating and Doing respectively. The sixth Sephira is on the central Pillar of Being. It represents the point where the mental being-ness of the Quantum God is located. In other words, the Quantum God occupies the sixth Sephira while determining his fixed attitudes and responses. But since the sixth Sephira is below the level of the fourth and fifth Sephiroth, the state of being which it represents is conditioned by them. In a way, the Quantum God builds himself a mental box into which he then crawls.

The sixth Sephira is the converging point between the Ontological Mind Triad (the conditioners of his mental being-ness) and the triad of the Corporal Mind (the mental aspect of the body or the body-mind). Here the Quantum God mediates the functioning of his subjective mind and the sensations, feelings, and emotions of his body. This Sephira represents the point of the incarnation of the Quantum God into the human body and the objective reality of the co-creation.

Here we must move to the World of the Body in order to describe the relationship between a Quantum God, his subjective mentality (as represented by the Ontological Mind Triad), and his physical body.

9
The World of Body

The Paramagnetic Fields of the Mind

The cells of the body die and are replaced with new growth. Every seven years, we are told, the body, is a brand new one. Yet each of us has a continuing sense of bodily identity. We each retain our likeness throughout our lives.

In the first nine months after conception the body grows from a single fertilized cell and evolves through many of the stages that our species as a whole went through on its way to becoming human. After we are born, our bodies grow to many times their size at birth. Yet during this amazing maturation period, from infancy to adulthood, our bodies retain their basic proportions.

Science attributes all this to the genetic codes which are held within the nucleus of each of the body cells. One can attribute much of this phenomenon of development to the function of the brain; but the brain also undergoes tremendous changes in the pre-birth period.

There is another way of seeing this. We normally think of the body as being the physical matter of which it is composed. But that is only one way of describing it. The body is also composed of fields of paramagnetic energy which act to attenuate matter and construct the physical body as we know it. These fields of energy act as templates which guide each step in the growth and development of the body, acting as patterns which guide its complex functioning.

In an earlier chapter, it was pointed out that matter and consciousness are really two aspects of the same thing. As matter evolved in complexity, beginning with the additional Thots about it which produced the qualities of time, space, energy, and mass, consciousness also 'complexified'. Mass is the quality which formalized matter into structured, functioning units such as molecules. Molecular consciousness evolved along with molecular matter to produce the highly complex, animal body-minds that we are familiar with today.

Both matter and consciousness evolved out of a field of energy of infinite proportions. Only a small percentage of the matter in the universe contains enough mass for us to consider it physical in nature (our use of the word 'physical' denotes matter in a relatively high mass condition). We know that if all the physical matter in the universe were spread evenly throughout space there would only be a few molecules of it every cubic mile. Physical matter is collected into large bodies such as planets and stars. These bodies contain most of the mass of the universe. But between them are vast distances where matter in a high mass condition hardly exists at all. The universe contains matter mainly in a mass-less condition which we call energy. This energy surrounds and interpenetrates all the physical matter of the universe.

We know that mass and energy are convertible factors. They are simply two conditions under which matter exists. Although one of these aspects may be more apparent in a particular case than the other, both exist together, whether we call it mass or energy. Electromagnetic matter-energy exhibits both mass and energy characteristics even though it is referred to as energy. The current terminology for units of electromagnetism is the wavicle, a combination of the particle-like aspect corresponding to mass and the wave-like aspect corresponding to the energy characteristic.

Everything electrical is accompanied by its magnetic component. Magnetism and electricity are convertible factors, just as mass and energy are. The magnetic component of electrical energy is its mass. The electrical component is energy. In its simplest form, mass is the pattern through which the energy moves. The wave pattern in electromagnetic propagation is the mass component. The capacity to do work is the energy component. The magnetic component is the path. We normally think of the magnetic field as the result of the activity of energy. But the reverse is also true since the magnetic field in which the energy is travelling determines the path configuration (a wave in the case of energy and an orbit in the case of the atom).

Atoms are called matter rather than energy since they have more mass, i.e. a more restricted path. Scientists utilize magnetic fields to accelerate atomic and sub-atomic particles, which are units of energy, and guide them to their targets in atomic accelerators. In summary, the magnetic field component of all energy phenomena determines how that energy manifests and is analogous to mass.

Moving up the scale of evolution of matter-consciousness, in the direction of complexity, we come to the body-mind. The body is a complex organization of energy transactions on many levels (electromagnetic, electrical, electrochemical, and chemical-mechanical). All body functions involve the ingestion, utilization and transformation of energy in one form or another. The body is the way a Quantum God handles the energy of the physical world. The body is the energy aspect of the body-mind.

The mind is the body's magnetic component. It is the field of paramagnetic (magnetic-like) matter which acts as magnetism does with respect to electrical energy. The paramagnetic field organizes the energy transactions of the body just as a magnetic field organizes electrical energy into wave patterns and orbits.

The paramagnetic field is composed of various frequencies or flux densities, each of which can be considered to be a separate field of its own. Yet all the frequencies of the field inter-penetrate each other and affect each other. The denser fields act as a holding pattern for the physical matter of the body. This is called the etheric body in most metaphysical systems. Another field inter-penetrates the etheric body or body pattern. This field is tuned to the emotional state of the individual. This is seen by sensitives as the aura, an egg-shaped field containing colours and shapes which surrounds the physical body. Another frequency of the field is attuned to the psychological functioning of the individual. It also affects the coloration and shapes within the aura.

The fields seem to originate from two different evolutionary directions. All the physical matter of the universe is structured by fields of energy. An atom is a particular kind of field. A cell has its typical kind of field. Seen as an assemblage of physical matter, the body has it own kind of field simply as a result of the

physical matter of which it is composed. Every chemical-electri-
cal activity of the physical body, then, affects the field configuration of the body in some way.

But other frequencies of the paramagnetic field are independent of the physical matter of the body. They originate with the
individual Quantum God occupying a body. A Quantum God
carries these fields with him from lifetime to lifetime. These
fields of energy have frequencies which overlap and inter-penetrate fields originating from the physical matter of the body.
While a Quantum God is in a physical body, the two sets of paramagnetic fields, one belonging to the Quantum God and the
other, originating from the physical matter of the body, interact
through a process of induction.

The Ability Domain

A Quantum God is not physical. The only way he experiences
anything is by connecting it directly with his Thot. To understand how a Quantum God experiences things from within his
body-mind (represented by the sixth Sephira) we can hypothesize
the following mental picture: let us imagine that surrounding a Quantum God is a spherical domain. We will call this the
domain of direct experience and action or the ability domain.
Within the ability domain a Quantum God knows things by
having the Thot that they exist, and creates things by the same
process. The domain of direct experience and action is the
'physical' manifestation of the World of Ability. Within the
ability domain, an individual is God. We can define God as one
who has direct experience and action within a particular domain.

Imagine that surrounding the ability domain is another
domain which is quite a bit larger. This larger domain is the
highest frequency of the paramagnetic field and is the 'physical'
manifestation of the Ontological Mind Triad (represented by the
fourth, fifth, and sixth Sephiroth in the World of Mind). This
field is the subjective mind. It acts as a buffer zone between the
Quantum God and his domain of direct experience and all the
other frequencies of the paramagnetic field including the
Corporal Mind field, the emotional field, the Body Pattern, and

the physical matter of the body. These 'lower' fields surround the sphere of the Ontological Mind which contains the domain of direct experience.

When a Quantum God takes an attitude, i.e. makes a decision to experience something in a particular way, his intentionality (Thot) causes a change in the field configuration of Ontological Mind. This change manifests as a constriction in the field surrounding his ability domain, which is the Ontological Mind. Since the Ontological Mind stands between the domain of direct experience and action and the other fields which compose his body, all the sensations, emotions, feelings, and thoughts originating in the physical body will be filtered by it. Conversely, the ability of a Quantum God to effect changes in his physical body and initiate action and responses will be inhibited by these same distortions in the field surrounding him.

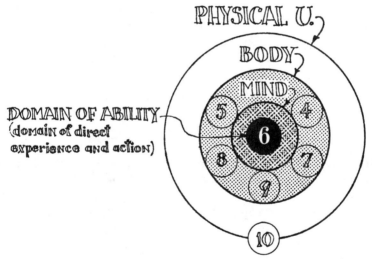

The diagram above shows the domain of ability contained within the sixth Sephira at the center. Surrounding the domain of ability is the domain of the subjective mind containing the Ontological Mind Triad above (the fourth, fifth, and sixth Sephiroth) and the Corporal Mind Triad below (the sixth, seventh, and eighth Sephiroth). Surrounding the subjective mind is the circle representing the body which intersects the ninth Sephira (representing the body-as-energy function). Surrounding the body is the circle representing the physical matter of the universe which intersects the tenth Sephira (representing matter).

The Body Tree

The Tree of Life does not lend itself easily as an accurate representation of the physiological form of the body. It is possible, though, to use it as a way of classifying, in a very general way, the functions of the body as they relate to the functions of the mind. The diagram (p. 195) shows the functions that are associated with conscious awareness in the body-mind.

The fourth and fifth Sephiroth, as a pair, represent the functions of the cerebral cortex. Physiologically, this is where sensation becomes conscious, memory is stored, and the voluntary muscles are consciously set into action. It also functions to hold together a coherent picture of reality, built up out of thousands of bits of sensory impulses from the body. It is here that the paramagnetic field which is the mind influences the way we perceive reality and respond to it.

The sixth Sephira in the World of Mind corresponds to the domain of direct experience and action at the center of the mental field. In the World of the Body, the sixth Sephira corresponds to the thalmic region of the brain. It is here that the Ontological and Corporal Minds overlap and are centered in the physical body. It is here that all the perceptions from the various senses of the body are made available to the Quantum God. It is in the thalmic region that the Quantum God simultaneously occupies his Worlds of Ability, Mind, and Body.

The thalmic region of the brain forms the axis around which the various parts of the brain are arranged in an arc. A line drawn through the spinal column extended upward would run right through the thalmic area. Adjacent to the thalmus is the pineal gland, the master gland of the endocrine system, which chemically regulates the growth and differentiation of the tissues of the body. A Quantum God located here tends to be visually oriented since the optic nerve is in close proximity.

Through the structure of the nervous system, sensations, feel-

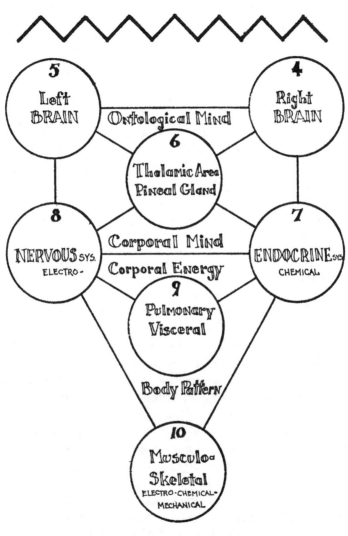

THE WORLD OF BODY

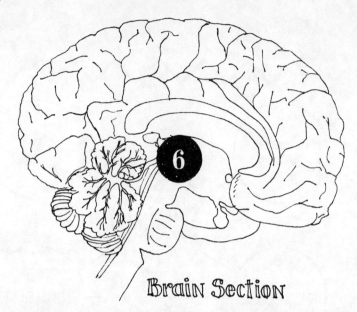

Brain Section

ings, and emotions which are, in the realm of the body, highly energetic phenomena, are reduced to millivolts of electrical impulse and are fed into the brain. In the brain, a Quantum God selects out of all the sensations available only the ones which he is willing to experience (allow into his domain of ability). He restricts the strength of the sensation impulses, and blocks out others, through the use of his mind (the paramagnetic field) which literally stands between him and his brain.

The consciousness of a Quantum God grows as he lets down the defenses (fixed attitudes) of his mind and allows more and more sensory experience to flow into his domain of direct experience. Subsequently, he becomes more and more able to respond directly from his body without the inhibitions of his mind getting in the way. The process of personal growth in consciousness is paralleled by the increasing size (with respect to his physical body) of his domain of direct experience and action.

With the Quantum God's dis-identification from his mind, and subsequently from his brain, he is able to move his domain of direct experience to other locations within the world of his body. There he can experience the activities of his body without having to rely on the abstracted interpretations of his brain. There are locations within the body which provide the Quantum God with whole other ranges of experience. These are the energy centers of the body which are called *chakras*.

At some point in the development of the Quantum God, he will occupy the whole of his body. Each cell of the body, each organ, including the brain, will be contained within the domain of direct experience. He will have fully incarnated into and become one with his body. This, I believe, is the state of consciousness referred to in the Bible as 'Christ'. The Quantum God will be as the 'Father within', while his body will function as 'His only begotten son'.

To complete the Tree of Life in the World of Body, as it relates to the physiology of the body, the four remaining Sephira must be described. The seventh Sephira corresponds to the endocrine system. It includes the pineal, thyroid, parathyroid, adrenal, reproductive glands, etc. These glands function to guide the growth of the body from a unicellular organism into a complete body. They provide the chemical environment, through the excretion of hormones, which regulates the relatively long-term processes of the body and, to some extent, regulate the function of the nervous system which works through the chemical environment of the body. Long-lasting emotional moods are also supported chemically by the endocrine glands.

The eighth Sephira represents the functioning of the body in its electrical aspect – the flow of electrical impulses through the nerves of voluntary, involuntary, sympathetic, and parasympathetic systems. While the endocrines control the chemical aspect of the body, the nervous system does so electrically and directs the relatively short-term functions of the body – sensations, reflexes, and movement.

The ninth Sephira represents the parts of the body which function as energy converters and energy storers. The digestive system and the pulmonary system function to take in and convert chemical energy, in the form of food, air, and water, into electrical energy, or another form of chemical energy. These systems function also to get rid of the by-products of energy utilization by excreting carbon dioxide and unusable chemical residue.

The tenth Sephira represents the skeletal-muscular systems which are dependent on the energy systems of the body for their functions as the converters of electro-chemical forms of energy into the mechanical energy of body movement. This Sephira also represents the physical matter of the universe as it is attenuated into the body pattern.

All these various aspects of the body energy process interact with all the others. There is no one function which is isolated from any other. This is true within the body, and between the body, mind, and the Quantum God within.

I will not attempt to classify the body further or relate it to the angels and powers which are assigned to the World of Yetzirah, which corresponds to the World of the Body in the model of Psychometaphysics. To do so would, I believe, have no usefulness. Science has accumulated a vast amount of knowledge concerning the functioning of the human body. This has been supplemented in recent years by the discovery of the fields of energy surrounding the body which I have referred to and which have been known to metaphysicians for centuries. To discuss the body and its energy fields in any detail would take another book. For further information, I refer the reader to the works of Wilhelm Reich (orgone energy), books by C. W. Leadbeater, and many others, on the subject of the energy centers of the body; also the many works in English on the science and practice of Acupuncture.

10
The Body-Mind

The World of Mind was set aside temporarily in order to describe the connection between the sixth Sephira and the physical body. The body-mind is represented by those Sephiroth which are below the sixth. These Sephiroth represent the functioning of a Quantum God who is located in the sixth Sephira, within his body-mind. More specifically, they represent an individual's subjective experience, as he functions in the world, through his individual mental and corporal universe, the universe of his body-mind.

The Ontological Mind Triad represents the effect of attitudinal viewpoints (fourth Sephira) and the ability to respond (fifth Sephira) which, together, establish a State of Being in the sixth Sephira. The Corporal Mind Triad represents thoughts and feelings which are derived from the body as experienced from the sixth Sephira. The Corporal Mind Triad represents the normal waking consciousness with which we are all familiar. The Corporal Mind Triad represents the contents of consciousness while the Ontological Mind Triad represents the state of consciousness from which we view them.

The Corporal Mind Triad

The Seventh Sephira: Feeling

Title of all No. 7 Sephiroth	Netzach, Victory
Yetziratic Appellation	The Occult Intelligence
Archangel	Haniel, The Grace of God
Symbol in Assiah	Venus

The derived meaning of the symbol for Venus is feeling. It indicates an awareness arising from within the body. The subjective experience of feelings is a result of energy transactions

within the body as perceived through the paramagnetic field of
the mind. The clearer the mind is, the more it allows feelings
and sensations to pass from the body into the consciousness of the
individual. The more attitudes a person has about things, the
less he will be in touch with his feelings.

Feeling is called the Occult Intelligence because it is another
mode of perception, one which is normally not conscious to the
average person. This is because we are taught to perceive the
world through our thoughts and to distrust our feelings. Feelings
are, by and large, considered to be irrational and a disturbance
to the rational thought processes which we tend to make sacred.
A sensitive person, however, can perceive an underlying reality
behind the thoughts and ideas of others. A sensitive person can
experience the world and others in much more of an immediate
and experiential way.

It has taken the universe millions upon millions of years to
develop a body which can give us a true picture of the universe as
it is. This picture is formed out of the sensations and feelings
which are delivered to us through our bodies. Sensation and feeling tell us what is going on within our bodies, between ourselves
and others, and our bodies and the rest of the universe. The only
thing which distorts this picture of reality is our thoughts about
it and the attitudes we have taken concerning it.

The Eighth Sephira: Conceptualization

Title of all No. 8 Sephiroth	Hod, Glory
Yetziratic Appellation	Absolute or Perfect Intelligence
Archangel	Raphiel, The Divine Physician
Symbol in Assiah	Mercury

The symbol for Mercury indicates a process whereby energy
or information coming from above passes through awareness
into fixity below. It is the same as the symbol for Venus except
that it indicates something received from above (indicated by
the receptive crescent). This Sephira arises out of the Sephira of
Feeling numerically, indicating its dependence on it. Feelings
arise out of the body while conceptualizations concerning those
feelings arise out of the mind. In other words, the way we conceive things is dependent on our state of being (sixth Sephira)

which is, in turn, dependent on our fixed attitudes (fourth Sephira) as they affect our ability to respond (fifth Sephira).

Conceptualization is a process of abstracting from sensual and feeling experience a symbol in the form of a word, an idea, or image representing that sensation or feeling. Concepts then become the currency of the mind and brain. This is a very important function since it enables us to think abstractly and communicate with each other. The problem occurs when we forget that concepts merely represent things and we begin to believe that the concepts are the things themselves.

Path No. 14, The Death of a Role

The fourteenth Path connects State of Being (sixth Sephira) with Feeling (seventh Sephira). It has been assigned the letter *noon*, the Death card in the Tarot, and the sign of Scorpio which means 'I desire'.

The state of being, or role that one is in, determines what one is sensitive to and what emotional reactions will be played out in any situation. A mother is sensitive to the crying of a baby as a person in no other role is. The role of child allows him to play and have uninhibited fun as no other state of being does. The role of victim makes a person sensitive to anything in the environment which can be interpreted as a threat and therefore used to reinforce the role. All roles have their attendant ranges of sensitivity to feelings and sensation. All roles have their sets of emotional reactions – the programs as to how one is to feel in a certain situation and how to respond to it.

The process also works in reverse. The state of being can be altered or radically changed by strong feelings or sensations. A child may suddenly be thrown into an adult role, for example as the 'invulnerable man', when he experiences some great disappointment or tragedy.

One way of interpreting the meaning of the Death card in the Tarot is that it indicates the death of a role we have created. Since the individual is identified with the role, or state of being, he will experience its loss as a personal death. The tragedy may simply be that someone has seen through one's façade and into the parts of oneself that the role has been hiding.

Path No. 16, The Use of Concepts

The sixteenth Path connects State of Being (sixth Sephira) with Conceptualization (eighth Sephira). It bears the letter *ayn*, the Devil card in the Tarot, and the sign of Capricorn whose key idea is 'I use'.

Conceptualization is a process of describing experience through the use of abstract symbols in the form of words or images. The choice of symbols, the words used to describe to oneself or others the experiences of life is dependent upon which state of being one is in at the time. We are all able, potentially, to utilize various sets of conceptual symbols to describe what happens to us or what we have observed. In the role of scientist a person will describe a flower differently from when in the role of poet. The concepts we use at any given time will reveal and reinforce the attitudes that constellate around the state of being we are in.

Paths number fourteen and sixteen, as a pair, indicate the ability of a Quantum God to produce thoughts and feelings in his body through his intentionality. We usually assume that we can have any thought we like since our education system places a lot of emphasis on our thinking abilities. We do not, however, usually assume that we can, at will, evoke feelings as well. This ability is normally developed by those in the theatrical professions. But all of us are actors and actresses with respect to the roles we play out in life (sixth Sephira). Although we may be unaware of it, we all evoke emotions as well as thoughts.

Path No. 17, Conceptualization of Feeling

The seventeenth Path connects Conceptualization (eighth Sephira) to Feeling (seventh Sephira). It bears the letter *phay*, the Tower card in the Tarot, and the symbol for Mars.

The way that feeling and sensation are conceptualized determines the way and degree to which an individual is conscious of them. We are all aware of feelings since the mind rarely keeps them from becoming conscious to some degree. Feelings are handled mentally by labelling them with concepts. We all know the meaning of the concept of sadness. But we are not usually conscious of the energy of sadness in our bodies and the effect that the energy or feeling has in various parts of our bodies. Every feeling or emotion has definite effects on our breathing, the muscular tension in specific parts of our bodies, and the associated feelings incorporated in the character structure which are activated when we feel sad. The label 'sadness' is just a label which hides us from the vast array or sensations and feelings which act together to produce it. The concept of sadness is a collective thought which prevents us from differentiating the various sensations and bodily effects which produce sadness. This lack of differentiation keeps us from feeling the full depth and quality of our feelings and emotions. Feelings are often mixed together. A feeling is often accompanied by other feelings, adding to the confusion of mind which prevents full conscious experience of body energy.

The Paths Connecting the Ontological and Corporal Mind Triads

The sixth Sephira stands at the intersection where Fixed Attitudes, Response-Ability, Feeling, and Conceptualization interact to reveal the role, or State of Being, that a Quantum God is in at any one time. In this way, the sixth Sephira acts as a Path connecting the Ontological and Corporal Mind Triads. There are two additional Paths which connect these triads. They are the eleventh and thirteenth. They do not connect to the sixth Path indicating that they function below awareness regardless of the state of being one is in.

Path No. 11, Emotionality

The eleventh Path connects Fixed Attitudes (fourth Sephira) to Feeling (seventh Sephira). It bears the letter *khaf*, the Wheel card in the Tarot, and the planet Jupiter.

This Path lies on the Pillar of Relating on the Tree of Life. Its location does not connect it to the State of Being, therefore it represents an unconscious mental function, one which a Quantum God occupying the central position of the mind is unaware of. While the tenth Path shows the influence of Fixed Attitudes on the State of Being, the eleventh Path shows the influence of Fixed Attitudes on feelings, emotionality, and sensations.

Feelings and emotions often seem to occur in a random fashion with respect to the situation at hand. In actuality, all emotional reactions, except the immediate and appropriate natural expression of a feeling, are patterned by the same fixed attitudes that condition the mental thought patterns. We could say that fixed attitudes place the feelings on the wheel of fixed reactivity. Free-flowing feelings thus become emotion. For example, a person who believes fervently in a fixed attitude about patriotism or religion will experience emotions of exaltation when someone praises his country or religion. Conversely, he may fly into a rage of anger when these beliefs are challenged or criticized. Jealousy and hostility towards anyone who pushes against one's attitudes about the possession of things and others are emotional patterns tied to basic psychological attitudes. They are not often overcome because, being so prevalent, they are part of the assumed, intrinsic nature of human beings as seen by many societies. The social reality often reinforces these attitudes.

The difference between a feeling and an emotion is this: feelings arise as a result of a change in the relationship between the energy system of one's body and the energy system of others. They are spontaneous perceptions and give rise to spontaneous responses. Emotions, on the other hand, are mentally controlled feelings which are not spontaneous and are entirely dependent on the fixed habit patterns of the mind. Rather than response, or direct action, they manifest as reactions and calculated attempts to manipulate others into doing what you want them to do by emotional intimidation.

People who are highly reactive emotionally cannot usually tell the difference between a spontaneous feeling perception and their mentally programmed reaction patterns. To them, feelings appear always as reactions, usually defensive ones. The use of the feelings as a mode of perceiving the state of relationship between them and others is lost. They depend entirely on their thought processes to analyze the emotions of themselves and others. This is because they are unwilling to experience their own feelings and express them to others.

Path No. 13, The Inconceivable

The thirteenth Path connects Response-Ability (fifth Sephira) with Conceptualization (eighth Sephira). It bears the letter *mem*, the Hanged Man in the Tarot, and the symbol of the planet Neptune.

The symbol for Neptune indicates a process of reception of information or energy which is fixed into a pattern without conscious mental awareness. It refers to the inability of an individual to make conscious to himself, i.e. have the thought of, some thing which lies outside his mental framework. This inability to respond to experience with the appropriate concept – with which mentally to understand it – is dependent on the quality and quantity of fixed attitudes and response-ability of the fourth and fifth Sephiroth respectively.

When an individual takes on an attitude about something or someone, he is, in effect saying he is unwilling to experience the opposite aspect of it. If someone decides to see his child as being good then he will refuse to experience the child's badness. It will be difficult even to conceive of the child as having bad qualities. The attitude which determines the response to another tends to block awareness of that which he is unwilling to experience and respond to.

The Corporal Energy Triad

The Ninth Sephira: Energy State

Title of all No. 9 Sephiroth	Yesod, Foundation
Yetziratic Appellation	Pure or Clear Intelligence
Archangel	Gabriel, The Man-God
Symbol in Assiah	The Moon

The sixth Sephira represents the influences that mentality has on the state of being of a Quantum God. The ninth Sephira, which is also located on the central Pillar of Being, represents the overall sensual-feeling condition of the body. It might be called the state of excitation of the body. It is the general state of the energy of the body.

The mental paramagnetic field surrounding and inter-pene-

trating the body determines how and to what degree energy from
the environment and others will flow through the body. The
flow of energy through the body activates feelings and thoughts
which are then filtered by the subjective mind and delivered to
the Quantum God within. Thus each state of being has its
accompanying energy state of the body.

Mentality acts as resistance to energy flow. Each attitude in the
mind restricts and inhibits energy flow in a specific way. Chronic
restrictions of energy flow manifest in the body as chronic muscular tensions and eventual disease. The more an individual values
his thoughts and devalues his feelings, the less energy his body
will have.

The Energy State is experienced subjectively as a sense of
bodily identity. The body is constricted in order to fit the self-
image or ego. Along with the self-image there is the attendant
set of muscular tensions which give the individual a sense of self.
Without these tensions the body is felt to be an integral part of
the universe. With these tensions, the body is experienced as
belonging to the individual, a thing separate from nature.

Path No. 15, Experiencing Energy

The fifteenth Path connects State of Being (sixth Sephira) to
Energy State (ninth Sephira). It is assigned the letter *sammekh*,
the Temperance card in the Tarot, and the sign of Sagittarius
which means 'I see'.

It is through the fifteenth Path that the Quantum God 'sees'
or experiences the energy of his body. Each state of being that a
Quantum God is in determines to some degree his capacity to experience and utilize the basic energy of his body. This energy is
basically sexual. We do not usually experience it as sexual except
in the sex act itself since our mental framework tends to change
(sublimate) it into moods, emotions, and reaction patterns. If we
could remove the constraints on our body energy that the mind
imposes we would experience sexual pleasure in the simple act
of breathing.

An example of how our mental structure distorts this basic
energy is as follows: Excitement is a sudden increase in the
amount of energy which is flowing through the body. Yet most of

us, when we experience excitement, react by taking an attitude towards it which distorts our subjective experience of it. We unconsciously slow our breathing as images arise in our mind which connect what is happening to other events in our lives and the attitudes we have taken in the past. We tense our muscles in an attempt to control the excitement. But in the act of controlling the excitement it is distorted. Instead, we experience fear or some form of paranoia. What might have been an exciting and pleasurable experience becomes one full of discomfort, and all our defense mechanisms come into play.

Path No. 18, The Feeling Perception

The eighteenth Path connects Feeling (seventh Sephira) with Energy State (ninth Sephira). It is assigned the letter *tsadde*, the Star card in the Tarot, and the sign of Aquarius which means 'I know'.
Knowledge is usually considered to be a function of conceptual thinking. But, in the realm of inter-personal relationship, this kind of knowledge is practically useless. What a person knows, or how much data is available to his memory, gives little indication as to what that person is like or how he feels about himself, life and others – including you. This kind of information comes not from the conceptual mind but from the feelings of the body.

When the conceptual mind is quieted a person can become aware of the effects that others have on him and his effects on others. The body is a highly tuned instrument. It tends to vibrate energetically with its environment and other people in the vicinity. The feeling of the city is a very different feeling from that of the country. A yellow flower has a different feeling from a red one. A rigid attitude-bound person feels very different from a relaxed, open person. On the energy level represented by the ninth Sephira, feelings are as distinct from one another as thoughts are.

This Path indicates the ability of the body to respond to and differentiate, the feeling environment. While the fourteenth Path indicates the ability of a Quantum God to create feelings in his body, the eighteenth Path indicates the ability of the body to evoke feelings on its own. These body-originated feelings give the Quantum God another mode of perception which is often more accurate and informative than his thoughts about things.

Path No. 20, Conceptualized Energy

The twentieth Path connects Conceptualization (eighth Sephira) to Energy State (ninth Sephira). It has been assigned the letter *raysh*, the Sun card in the Tarot, and the symbol for the Sun.

This Path indicates the ability of the body to evoke conceptual thoughts in the mind. While the sixteenth Path indicates thoughts arising from the intent of the Quantum God, this Path indicates thought arising from the body. Through the Paths connecting with the ninth Sephira, the body has the ability to produce thoughts and feelings which are essential to its survival and well being.

When the body requires food it produces feelings and thoughts which grow in strength until they are recognized and acted upon by the individual. The body has an amazing intelligence of its own. Its messages to the mind of the individual contain all the necessary information for maintaining health. If the individual is in tune with his body, he will always know exactly what to eat and how much.

The Body Pattern Triad

The Tenth Sephira: Personality

Title of all No. 10 Sephiroth	Malkuth, Kingdom
Yetziratic Appellation	The Resplendent Intelligence
Archangel	Sandalphon, The Messiah
Symbol in Assiah	The Earth

The tenth Sephira represents the *gestalt* of all the other Sephiroth and Paths acting as a unity. The symbol for the Earth is a cross within a circle. The arms of the cross divide the circle into four quarters. The four arms represent the four-fold process of the Tetragrammaton. The four quadrants represent the spiritual, mental, emotional, and corporal aspects of the individual. The circle enclosing the cross indicates these aspects functioning as a unity, the personality.

Many people who are on a spiritual quest of some sort consider the personality to be something other than spiritual. They believe that one can get rid of the personality or ego and live entirely as a spiritual being. They imagine that the spirit is something separate from the ego or personality. Certainly we should all strive to rid ourselves of any images and attitudes which we feel do not express our inner nature. Many others confuse the real Self with the ego or personality and assume that, when these two have been eliminated, there is no self left. But, after all attitudes and images are given up, the Self continues to manifest in the world of human beings.

Every aspect of an individual, including the shape of his body, is a product of the spiritual Self, the Quantum God. When you are having a conversation with someone, you are talking to a Quantum God. When someone takes your hand, you are being touched by a Quantum God. When you look into a mirror you are looking at a Quantum God. 'But that is just my body and personality,' you might reply. Yet that is just your attitude. The Quantum God is not just a point in spiritual space; it includes everything you think, do, or say.

Path No. 19, Instinct

The nineteenth Path connects Feeling (seventh Sephira) with Personality (tenth Sephira). It bears the letter *qof*, the Moon card in the Tarot, and the sign of Pisces which means 'I believe'.

A belief in the mental context is a decision to take an attitudinal viewpoint towards something. In the body, however, beliefs manifest as fixed emotional feeling states which are deeply subconscious reaction patterns, called instincts. An instinct is a bodily belief in a way of being and doing which has helped the body in the past in its fight for survival. These instinctive beliefs are so common among humans that they are considered to be part of human nature.

If we place the beliefs of the mind against the beliefs of the body, we can see the basic dichotomy between the material and spiritual natures of mankind. The highest intellectual aspirations of sane, rational behavior are often overwhelmed by the material need to survive in any way possible. Conversely, the necessity for survival is superseded occasionally by trans-personal aspirations, such as saving the life of another whilst endangering one's own.

We may imagine that these two forces oppose each other and that one is more spiritual than the other. But the instinct to survive is a reflection in the body of the spiritual intent of a Quantum God to Be and continue to Be. The drive of sexuality, also considered to be a bodily instinct is a reflection of the spiritual intent of a Quantum God to contact and experience another, and to do so in the act of co-creation (procreation).

Path No. 21, Awareness of Self

The twenty-first Path connects Conceptualization (eighth Sephira) to Personality (tenth Sephira). It bears the letter *sheen*, the Judgement card in the Tarot, and the planet Pluto.

The way we conceive ourselves to be is often different from how we really are in the world. This is because we have the ability to control the degree to which we are aware of ourselves. If we have preconceived ideas or beliefs about how we should be, we tend to judge ourselves in terms of whether or not we are living up to these beliefs. This leads to the common syndrome of trying to improve the *way* we are, without first becoming aware of *how* we are in the present.

The character structure through which we express ourselves is the result of the way we have created our own personal reality. It is important to remember that what exists in the present is a result of one's inner creative activities of the past. Before a new and better creation can replace an old one there must be an awareness of what exists in the present. The manifestation of past creativity must be accepted into awareness since awareness of what has been created is the last step in the creative process. By not accepting the present state of things, you are denying your responsibility for having created it and are impairing your ability to respond with new and better creations.

By standing back and judging yourself, while not accepting how you are now, you will find yourself in a double bind. By wilfully trying to force yourself into fitting an image in your mind, you are fighting yourself. It becomes a battle of inner creativity versus outer discipline, the struggle of humanity.

Path No. 22, The Material Medium

The twenty-second Path connects Energy State (**ninth Sephira**) with Personality (tenth Sephira). It bears the letter of *tav*, the World card in the Tarot, and the symbol of Saturn.

This Path, as with all Paths, is a two-way street. In the passive or receptive mode, energy is derived from the **matter of the** physical universe (another aspect of the tenth **Sephira**). Energy enters the body-mind in the form of food which is organic material held together by chemical bonds. The **digestive system** releases the bond energy and makes it available **for use in the** body-mind. Energy is taken in from the air **in the form of** oxygen, which is necessary for metabolic processes, **and in the** form of ambient life force. Matter is taken in to the body and used to rebuild cells and provide for growth.

In the active mode, the physical matter of the **body provides a** means of interacting with the stuff of the physical **universe and** other individuals. Without the physical body **and the** senses, a Quantum God would be out of touch with the **objective reality** which is shared between all beings of the physical **universe. His** reality would be purely mental and there would **be no** way to test his subjective impressions of things with their **sensual reality.**

The physical reality provides a context of objectivity in which one Quantum God can communicate in a specific, differentiated, and conscious way with others. The conditions **of time, space,** energy, and mass, which the Quantum Gods place on the matter of the physical universe, act both as limitations **on a Quantum** God's abilities and a framework in which to **experience the** efficacy of all Thots, thoughts, feelings, and actions.

Matter is the great equalizer. Just imagine what **would happen** if we lived in a universe without the restrictions that matter imposes on us. Imagine what it would be like if **every thought** you had instantly came true. If you had a thought **about yourself** it would instantly change you into that image. **And what about** the thoughts you have about others? All of us **at one time or** another have had the thought of doing harm to others, or wishing for an instant that they were dead. Imagine **killing your best** friend in a fit of anger.

In some ways it would be nice to be free of **the physical re-** strictions. We could instantly travel to any place we **could think** of. We could fly if we wished. But the purpose of life is not to become supermen. The purpose of life is to become ever more conscious of our own nature and that of others. Therein lies the function of matter.

PART THREE
ENLIGHTENMENT
INTENSIVE

11
Enlightenment, the
Direct Experience of Truth

Introduction

All models, regardless of their accuracy, are mental constructs. As mental constructs they can only point to the truth. The truth, in an absolute sense, is only found *after* all mental constructs are transcended. The truth is that which is experienced directly from one's total being, without the limitations of conceptual thought or emotional reactions based on programs of the personal character structure. Once clear of these obstructions the truth is immediate, self-evident, and always in the here and now.

To many, the model, in which they have invested their belief, is the truth itself. These are the religious models. They are true simply because they are believed to be true. The Qabalah is seen by many in this way. But the Qabalah has been presented here in a different sense. For me, as suggested above it is just another mental construct around the truth and not the truth itself, in the absolute sense. Unlike most religious models the Qabalah offers a map of reality leading up to the truth. It is a method as well as a map. It is a way of approaching the truth by helping one to test and resolve every concept and feeling which may be inhibiting direct experience of truth. Like all mental constructs the Qabalah too must, in the end, be transcended.

There are hundreds of paths to take on the way to the truth. All of them have their validity and their time. Each person has his or her own individual path since the living of life, and all that is encountered in it, is, in a very real sense, the only path. The way in which each of us lives, experiences, and conceives of life is unique. Whatever maps or models we believe in represent the way we have chosen to conceive of ourselves. But Life itself has no fixed or ultimate roads which must be travelled; it is our beliefs, and our beliefs alone, that dictate our paths.

The problem with all the models and mental constructs concerning life is that a person has to invest faith in them. This is necessary and useful for a time since, without faith, the model would be useless as a path of growth. There comes a point, however, in personal growth, when the model has served its temporary purpose as a map and method. When this point arrives the individual must be ready to set the model aside and rely only on his inner being for the last part of the journey. This is a frightening thing for most of us. It requires a leap from the secure world of mental construct into the mental void of direct experience. If the model of reality that has brought us to that point is accurate enough, it will have given us the means to bring back into the everyday world the things that we have learned in the world of direct experience. If the model of reality that we have believed in is too distant from the truth, we may find ourselves denying our direct experience and reverting to the security of beliefs. Or we may distort the truth to fit our beliefs.

Few of us make the jump beyond our beliefs. Most of us do not even believe that this is possible. We remain in a world where belief is substituted for the truth. This is true for those of us who hold scientific beliefs as well as religious ones, for in this sense they are all religious in nature.

For me the path leading out of mental construct and into the world of direct experience has been a method, derived from Zen meditation, called the Enlightenment Intensive. It was through the Enlightenment Intensive that my belief in the Qabalah as truth itself was transcended. And it was through experience of the Enlightenment Intensive that I was able to formulate the model of Psychometaphysics described in Part Two.

The Enlightenment Intensive format was put together by Charles Berner, founder of the Institute of Ability in Lucerne Valley, California. Charles (who had studied Zen Buddhism for many years) and his wife Ava, were using a diad situation in which two people would face each other and ask each other various questions concerning their relationship. It occurred to Charles in the last months of 1968 that the same format might be used to answer the many *koans* (questions) with which he was familiar through his study of Zen. Charles called his students together and assigned them the question, 'Who am I?'. He was as surprised and happy as anyone to find that within a period of just a few days his students were having enlightenment experiences identical to the ones described by those who had been practising Zen meditation for up to ten years.[19]

It was during Charles' second Enlightenment Intensive that I discovered my own nature and the nature of life.

It was a five day Intensive and it changed my life considerably.

It is important here to point out to the reader that my interest in the inner workings of things, and the model of Psychometaphysics which I described in Part Two, is merely a side-line compared to the enlightenment experience itself. Most of the people who have participated in an Enlightenment Intensive (there have been thousands in both North America and Europe) are not concerned with the ultimate nature of reality. Their interest is in gaining the most valuable of all things – a direct experience of their own nature without the necessity of taking drugs, believing in some dogma, or spending two weeks to ten years in a Zen monastery.

The people who have participated are not extraordinary people. They have been of all ages, from all walks of life, and all sections of society and culture. The thing that is common to all of them is that they have a sincere desire to know the truth. Almost all of them are slightly skeptical in the beginning, as I was when I went to my first one. The hardest thing for us to overcome in the beginning is that awful word 'enlightenment'. It has so many bad connotations that it makes most people cringe when they hear it. But there is no other word in English that is accurate. I hope that the following description will clear the air of the many misunderstandings concerning it.

Enlightenment literally means to bring the light of consciousness into something. Enlightenment is experienced when you bring your full consciousness into direct contact with the truth. Enlightenment can occur to anyone in any circumstances in normal life and often does. The difference between enlightenment and an insight is that an insight is a mental phenomenon whereas enlightenment affects the entire being. An individual can have various kinds of enlightenment (enlightenment about the nature of the self or enlightenment about the nature of a flower) and varying degrees of enlightenment (superficial to very deep).

The key word in the statement above is *direct*. Direct, in this context, means 'without any by-way-of'. Normally we experience ourselves, life, and others by seeing, thinking, believing, deciding, reasoning, or feeling them. These are all indirect means of experiencing. Yet most of us assume that these are the only ways we can experience anything.

Enlightenment is a direct experience of the truth. The truth is that which exists apart from our perception or conception of it. In the case of self-enlightenment, it means that you are in direct contact with the truth of your 'I'. The previous sentence seems to suggest that there are two 'I's'. This is simply a result of our language and not the case in actuality. It might be said better this way: in the case of self-enlightenment you are at one with your 'I' in the sense of being your true 'I' consciously. In the state of enlightenment there is no mental dichotomy, no subject-object, but an at-one-ness with yourself. Perhaps this is what is meant by the word atonement (at-one-ment) found in scripture.

The Enlightenment Intensive is, of course, not the only way of gaining enlightenment. The first well-documented enlightenment was that of the Buddha. Buddhism has as its purpose the gaining of enlightenment through the methods used by the Buddha. There are also stories of enlightenment experience found in the biographies of Christian mystics and saints. The Hebrew name Aaron indicates the state of enlightenment. Other religions also have stories which tell of it and describe methods, such as yoga and meditation, which help to attain it. In recent times drugs such as mescalin and L.S.D. have been used to produce states of consciousness similar to, or the same as, that of enlightenment.

Most methods used in the past are based on isolating the seeker from the world. Self-enlightenment has and can be obtained simply (not necessarily easily or quickly) by isolating oneself from all outside influence. By removing the disturbances of others and all outside influences the seeker will find that he will eventually gain a deep experience of 'being alone' with himself, and come to know directly the feeling of who he is. Difficulty will arise, however, when the seeker comes back from isolation and re-contacts the world and interacts again with others. In the world, the seeker may find that his enlightenment remains only as a memory.

Enlightenment gained through the use of drugs such as L.S.D. is most often a temporary one. Although drugs can produce alternative states of consciousness including states of enlightenment, they, too, have the effect of isolating the individual from the 'normal world'. When the drug wears off, so does the experience. Again the enlightenment becomes a memory.

The Enlightenment Intensive is not a method of isolation. On the contrary, it is done with a number of people who interact with each other. It is this factor of relating directly to others that makes the E.I. unique. Since the enlightenment is achieved in the presence of others, there is less tendency for the experience to be lost and remain only as a memory. Enlightenment in this context, becomes lasting and practical.

People who are enlightened speak from their deepest source. They are no longer identified with being a role, such as a father or mother or child, or with a career such as a cab driver or diplomat, or with just their thoughts or emotions or with just their bodies. They may continue to do the normal things in life, but with a continuing awareness that they are more than any of these things. Such people speak from themselves without having to refer to the past thoughts of themselves or of others.

An enlightened person is more able to overcome consciously the circumstances in life that impede fulfilment and happiness. He thinks, feels, and acts from himself, throwing off more and more the shackles of his conditioning. He increasingly sees each moment in life as a new and unique experience and does not tend to be stuck in a limited way of seeing things.

Through life-enlightenment, a person gains a deeper sense of value for the living of a fuller life. He begins to see that life can be lived in a more fulfilling and alive way than he has ever dreamt of before. The dead humdrum, that most of us call living, is set aside. The compulsive yearning for objects and money as the way to gain happiness becomes secondary to the growing interest in deeper contact with life and others.

In the experience of another, the seeker finds a being equivalent in nature to himself, with the same basic nature and having the same basic needs; equivalent in nature yet in himself a totally unique individual. A new respect grows for all other human beings; a new understanding grows of the effects he has on others and the effects others have on him. The direct experience of another is one of life's most fulfilling experiences.

The Enlightenment Intensive itself is not a problem-solving device as many forms of therapy tend to be. What it does is to bring the participant into full conscious awareness of who he is in the present, here and now. The participant need not change one iota to become enlightened. Changes take place naturally after the enlightenment experience.

To say that a person can gain enlightenment in just three days is not entirely accurate. All that a person has experienced concerning the question he is working on (such as 'Who am I?') during his life up to that point is revealed to him in one instant during the experience.

Often people tell me after their experience that they knew it before. The difference is that this time they experienced it with their whole being. It was no longer just a thought they occasionally had.

Of course, the only real way to understand what enlightenment is, is to experience it for oneself. The best I can do to help get the idea across in words is to describe what actually goes on in an Enlightenment Intensive. Although the process is contracted into a short period of time (as short as three days), whatever the method of enlightenment used the stages gone through will be similar.

The Enlightenment Intensive Format

A group of people ranging in number from twelve to as many as eighty arrive somewhere in the countryside on the evening of the day before the Enlightenment Intensive begins. They have brought sleeping bags or bedding of some kind, a towel, a tooth-brush, comfortable clothing, and perhaps a pillow to sit on. They have left at home all drugs, including tobacco and alcohol, shaving equipment or make-up kit, and hopefully, all preconceived ideas.

Depending upon the facilities available, they will be sleeping and eating in the same room or rooms together. When they arrive someone will greet them, offer them a cup of soup or herbal tea, and urge them to get some sleep. The Intensive will begin at 6.00 a.m. the following day.

At six o'clock, the gentle sound of a bell or gong awakens the participants. They are told that we will all meet in the largest room in fifteen minutes. They are asked not to spend too much time in the bathroom, since there are often many people and few bathrooms.

At 6.15, the last of the sleepy-eyed participants assemble in the meditation room. The enlightenment master, who is to be the guide for what follows, is waiting there to welcome them and tell them about the process upon which they are to embark.

While they have been waiting for the last person to arrive, they may have taken the opportunity to introduce themselves to each other. It will be the only time during the Intensive that the participants will use each others' names.

'Good morning,' says the master. 'During the next three days, we will be working toward gaining a direct experience of the nature of our selves, life and others. It will help you at this point to decide that you can and will succeed in this effort. This decision will make it easier for you to put aside any doubts you have about whether or not it is possible for you to be enlightened through this process.

'Enlightenment is a very simple thing; it is the direct experience of the truth. By "direct" I mean without sensing, feeling, or thinking about it. Words are inadequate to convey my meaning. but you will know what I mean when you yourself have experienced it.

'I ask you now to put aside for these three days all outside thoughts. If there is any thing such as a telephone message or letter which must be received or sent by you, please let my assistants stand in for you. All incoming messages, unless they are concerned with some emergency, will be held for you until the end of the Intensive. It is important that you are not distracted by any outside disturbances. Is there anyone who feels that they must interrupt the Intensive for any reason?'

Occasionally people do not realize that the Intensive ends late on the third day and need to be found a ride home with one of the other participants.

'I ask you to put aside any skeptical attitude you may have, or any pre-conceived ideas, concerning the nature of enlightenment, or the answer to your question. Even if you already have an answer, or are correct in your estimation of what enlightenment is, the experience of it is quite different from the knowing of it.

'My purpose here is to encourage you to put every last ounce of effort into gaining your enlightenment. I can help you through some of the barriers you will encounter on the way and make sure that you achieve the deepest possible experience of enlightenment and not just an insight or an emotional catharsis.

'Some of you may find that you have difficulty with my authoritarian role here, or the highly-structured method that we are using. Please feel free to come and talk to me about this should it occur. The intensive structure that we will be using provides a format which optimizes the possibility that you will experience the truth of yourself, life, and others, rapidly and deeply. The format has worked for hundreds of people and it will work for you if you devote yourself to it fully.

'Before I explain the structure itself I would like to acquaint you with the rules. I ask you not to take any drugs, including tobacco and alcohol, tea and coffee, for the next three days; and not to eat anything other than what we serve you. You may drink water when you like. The diet is specially prepared from organic foods when possible, and both the quantity and quality assure you adequate nourishment during your physical and mental efforts here.

'If you wear glasses or contacts try, when working with your partner, taking them off. If you can see your partner in front of you without too much strain, work without your glasses as much as you can. Sometimes your vision will change for the better during this process since the way you see is often connected with some of the attitudes you hold concerning yourself and others.

'If any of you have an intimate relationship with anyone here I ask you not to work with each other until you consult with me. Couples almost always work on their relationship rather than the question. This is important for all of you: do this for yourself because *you* want to. If you are here because someone told you to, or if you are doing it for someone else, you're here for the wrong reasons and should consider coming back another time.

'I ask you not to have any sexual intercourse during the three days, and to refrain from masturbation. Put all your energy into what you are doing here.

'I urge you to speak in your own native language during the communication exercises, even if you are fluent in English and have spoken it for some time. Many of your attitudes concerning yourself were gained in childhood and are connected with the language you spoke then.'

The master will then help people who speak other languages find those who can understand their native tongue. I can recall an Intensive in which five languages were being spoken in the same room.

'When we begin I will assign to you the question that you will contemplate. It is important that you do not change the wording of your question, or the question itself, without first talking to me about it. The questions that we will be using are basically three: "Who am I?", "What is life?", and "What is another?"

'The communication exercise works like this: To begin each communication exercise I will tell you to find a partner. Try to work with a different person each time. You and your partner will sit down either on a chair or a cushion facing each other, a comfortable distance apart. Be sure that you are at the same eye level with each other. Sit facing each other as comfortably and relaxed as possible, but make sure that your back is straight. If you are comfortable in the lotus sitting position used in Zen, fine; if not, place your legs in any position that is comfortable preferably with your knees below your hips. Feel free to change your position when you like.

'The next instruction will be to find out from your partner

which question he or she is working on. Then I will ask one of you to give your partner the instructions. The statement you will make to your partner is not a question but a command. If your partner is working on the question, "Who am I?", then you will say, "Tell me who you are." Whatever question your partner is working on you will always say, "*Tell me* what life is", or "*Tell me* what another is", etc. Please hold to these exact words; not "Hey, Fred, who are ya?"

'The person who has been given the instructions then sets about experiencing himself, life or another – depending on which question he or she is working on. It is important that you take a few seconds to contemplate your question before answering your partner. When something occurs to you as a result of contemplating your question – whether it is a thought, a feeling, or a sensation; whether or not it seems to answer the question – tell your partner about it and, if it is a feeling, express it.

'The partner who has given the instructions then gives his full attention to his partner. He is to remain silent and do nothing but understand what his contemplating partner tells him. Do not try to help your partner or seek to agree or disagree with what he or she tells you. You can help him only by being there for him and understanding him as fully as you can. You are not to have a conversation, ask each other any questions, argue or encounter each other in any way during the Intensive. The only verbal communication allowed during the Intensive is during the communication exercise.

'At the end of five minutes you will hear a gong and one of my assistants or I will instruct you, "Thank your partner." This is simply to communicate appreciation to each other, one for having listened and one for having talked. You may wish to say thank you verbally, or with a nod of the head, or any way that feels appropriate to you at the time.

'Immediately following that instruction, you will be instructed to "change over". At that time, you simply reverse roles. The partner who has already given the instructions is now given his instructions by his partner.

'You will take turns like this, each turn lasting five minutes, for a total of forty minutes. At the end of the forty minutes, you will hear two sounds of the gong and the instructions to thank your partner and take a five minute rest or to begin some other activity. You will have the opportunity to work with each of the other participants during the Intensive.'

The master will then describe the day's activities. He points out to the participants that the schedule and format are designed with only one thing in mind; helping the seeker to take his or her mind off everything except the question he or she is working on. The participants are told that, if they need a tissue or a glass of water during a communication exercise, they should raise their hand and it will be brought to them. If they have any problem with their relationship with any of their partners, they are asked to talk to the master and not confront their partners personally about it. He urges them to be as considerate as possible to each other.

The typical first day's schedule is as follows:

6.00 –	6.15	Arise and dress
6.15 –	7.00	Opening lecture by the master
7.00 –	7.15	Breathing exercises
7.15 –	7.30	Tea
7.30 –	8.15	Communication exercise
8.15 –	8.45	Breakfast, vitamins
8.45 –	9.30	Communication exercise
9.30 –	10.15	Communication exercise
10.15 –	11.15	Walking contemplation
11.15 –	12.00	Communication exercise
12.00 –	12.45	Lunch, vitamins
12.45 –	13.30	Communication exercise
13.30 –	14.15	Lecture by master
14.15 –	14.45	Sitting contemplation
14.45 –	15.30	Communication exercise
15.30 –	15.45	Snack, vitamins
15.45 –	16.45	Working meditation
16.45 –	17.30	Rest
17.30 –	18.15	Communication exercise
18.15 –	19.15	Dinner, vitamins
19.15 –	20.00	Communication exercise

20.00 – 20.45   Communication exercise
20.45 – 21.45   Walking contemplation
21.45 – 22.30   Communication exercise
22.30 – 22.45   Hatha Yoga
22.45 – 23.00   Snack
23.00 – 23.45   Communication exercise
23.45 – 24.00   Retire
24.00 – 6.00   Sleeping contemplation

The schedule varies slightly as determined by the master. I myself have made continuous changes by varying the time of working meditations, walks, rest times, etc., according to the time of year and physical circumstances.

The diet is an organic vegetarian one, supplemented with natural vitamins. The diet contains, ideally, no sugar or processed foods, little or no milk products and very little spice or seasoning. The vitamins – such as C, B 12, B complex, D, B3, calcium, and tissue salts – are added to help under the rigorous conditions of the Intensive.

The master continues with his opening lecture: 'While you are doing the communication exercises, my assistants (helping to run the Intensive are either other Enlightenment Intensive masters, or students in training) and I will walk around the room and occasionally stop to listen to you. This is to be sure that you are doing the exercise properly and to assist you with any questions you may have concerning the structure of the exercise. They will also remind you to keep your back straight.'

The master will end his opening talk with a word of encouragement or perhaps an appropriate Zen story. Then there will be some breathing exercises to wake up and energize the body, followed by a cup of herbal tea.

The first communication exercise begins. Participants are told to work on the question, 'Who am I?' It is during the first communication exercise that those who have already been to an intensive and have answered this question are interviewed and given another question to work on.

The master may have already interviewed participants the night before and assigned them questions. Sometimes, especially in the case of an overly intellectual participant, the master will have the participant work on the alternative question, 'What is my true nature?'

During the first interview, the master will ask each participant if he or she has a history of mental illness, or has experienced the symptoms of schizophrenia. It is, however, quite unusual for a person who is extremely out of balance mentally to attempt an Enlightenment Intensive. The master will ask anyone whom he determines unable to do the Intensive to leave and may recommend someone who can help him. For those who have a tendency to de-personalize (a symptom of schizophrenia in which the person experiences a separation from his bodily existence), the master will add to his diet a special supplement of nicotinic acid (vitamin B3), which has been found effective in clearing the brain of the toxicity which can cause dissociation. Vitamin C is added with the B3 to improve the overall effects. For a person who is prone to extreme anxiety, calcium supplements are often effective. During the Intensive, the master will be aware of the predisposition of these participants and be ready to help them through these barriers to enlightenment.

The first day of the Enlightenment Intensive is usually the hardest of all. Most of us are not used to concentrating our attention on any one thing for any long period of time. As the day wears on, participants will find barriers arising which must be overcome in order to continue. By the middle of the day, the master will again lecture on the Intensive and the barriers that will be encountered.

'In all methods of enlightenment there are barriers to be found. The Enlightenment Intensive is no different; whatever barriers exist between you and your direct experience of you will arise here as well. I will tell you in a moment the stages that most people go through as they do the Intensive format.

'But, first, I must warn you that some of you during the first day may decide that this process is not working for you, or that it is not possible to succeed in this way. You may find it disconcerting not to be allowed to carry on normal conversations and get to know each other in a normal conversational way. Our purpose in doing this exercise is not to get to know each other – although that will also occur in a unique way – but to gain a direct experience of yourself. This is a very solitary undertaking.

'All of us have resistances which act as barriers to our doing what we have set out to do. I want you to consider all these resistances or barriers to be a direct result of what you are doing here. They arise because you are pushing on them. When these things stop you from continuing, please come and talk to me about them, and I will try to help you through them.

'See if you can understand the barriers in a different way. A barrier is actually something about yourself that you have not fully experienced and acknowledged as being a part of you. In this way you can see that what you call a barrier is something worth knowing about and experiencing. And that is the solution to the problem of barriers. Whatever comes into your consciousness, as a result of contemplating your question, must be fully and consciously experienced by you, and then communicated to your partner in enough detail for your partner to understand exactly what you are thinking and feeling. If this is done, then things will change and new thoughts and feelings will arise. You will have passed *through* the barrier without going around it or suppressing it.

'Some of the barriers you will encounter include tiredness, hunger, stiffness or aching in the body, a temporary inability to keep your mind on the question, and emotions and thoughts which you may not like to have. It is important, when they occur to you, to describe them to your partner in detail, as accurately as you can. Feelings are important in this respect. When you are having a feeling or emotion express it and describe exactly what it feels like to you. To say to your partner "I'm sad" is not enough. What does sadness feel like to you? Where does it occur in your body? How big is it? Does is suggest a color or shape to you? What thoughts enter your mind as you feel it?

'All feelings, emotions, and sensations should be handled in this way. In the case of anger, you may have the inclination to tell your partner that you are angry with him. You will think of some rational reason for getting angry with him, such as noticing that he is not listening to you as you think he should, or perhaps you suddenly don't like his face or the way he combs his hair. But the anger has arisen because you are pushing through your own emotions. Do not use your partner as a target for these feelings. Own them. Say that you are angry. Scream and yell your anger out, or beat on the cushion if you like, but do not direct it at anyone personally. You may think that you are angry at me or the process itself. In that case come and tell me about it. But, first, express it to your partner and then, if it persists, come to me.

'Now I want to tell you about the stages of enlightenment. They are the same for any method but in the intensive they will occur more quickly. The first stage is concerned with giving answers. In this stage, you will consider the question you are working on to be simply that – an intellectual question and you giving your partner answers. The answers you give are the ones you have learned from parents, teachers, priests and friends, or from things that you have read or heard someone say. They include also those answers you have already figured out in the past. By presenting these answers to your partner they will be cleared from your mind. It can take from two hours to over two days for some to go through this stage.

'Stage two is the intellectualizing stage. In this stage you will think things out logically and reasonably. If this is true, then that must be true, and so on. Sometimes in this stage you may come upon the "correct" answer. But since answers, correct or otherwise, are not what we are looking for you must continue to seek a direct experience of the truth of you. This stage is finished when you stop trying to answer a question and begin to set about to experience it directly.

'Stage three is the stage of phenomena. In this stage you will have been using your brain to such a degree that it will begin to produce unfamiliar mental and physical phenomena. Visions may appear. Hallucinations similar to those induced by psychedelic drugs may occur. The room may appear to distort. You may see auras around people and things. You may experience hot and cold flashes or waves of emotion running through your body. You may mistake these things for enlightenment. When I interview someone in this stage he may tell me "I am a bursting sun!" I will then ask him "who is perceiving it?"

'Stage four is the void. In this stage you will find your field of consciousness empty. No thoughts occur to you and no progress appears to be being made. At this stage I will review with you very carefully exactly how you are doing the exercise. To make further progress you must stop "looking" for yourself and seek to experience yourself directly, without "looking".

'Stage five is one in which you will encounter the barriers of emotion, pain, and death. You will experience feelings of fear, anger, grief, sadness, apathy, and serenity. In this stage, the states of being you have identified yourself with will come up and be expressed. These feelings are part of your character structure and keep you from feeling yourself as you actually are. They are constructs which may have, at some time, protected you from feeling something you did not want to feel and established an emotional sense of self which you have identified as being you. The feeling of death, or fear of death, arises as you dis-identify with these mental-emotional ego states. In some cases, where the enlightenment is going very deep, you must literally be willing to die in order to find out who you really are. I would like to assure any of you who go through this that no one has actually died during an Enlightenment Intensive.

'Stage six is the enlightenment experience itself. Two things occur simultaneously. First you will have a direct conscious experience of yourself and, second, you will experience a release of energy and other side effects. It occurs in a timeless instant. You will know it as a definite breakthrough. There will be no doubt in your mind. You may laugh, cry, scream or feel ecstasy. Some even have an orgasm. It is different for different people and for different depths of enlightenment.

'The seventh stage is the glow in which you are radiating yourself as truth. You will feel totally in contact with yourself and your presence will radiate from you like a glow. This will continue until you have fully presented yourself to others. The Zen people refer to this as "the Zen stink".

. 'Stage eight is the pure steady state. Once the energy is discharged, you will be in a steady state of being, able to present your true self to others and be in contact with it directly. The steady state will continue into your life to the degree that you continue to present the true you to others. In the pure steady state of consciousness of yourself, as you truly are, your interests will turn to life and others.

'And when your interests turn to life and others, I'll be here to give you your next question. It is not rare for someone to go through several questions in one Enlightenment Intensive. It only takes a split second.'

The lecture ends with a few words of encouragement and one can see in the faces of some of the participants a recognition that they have been through one or more of the stages that have been described. It is time now for a sitting meditation and the participants are asked to find a place in the room where they can sit comfortably and contemplate their question in silence.

The participants are told that, when a distracting thought occurs or when they mentally wander from the question, they are to simply bring their attention back to the question. The greater part of the first day is concerned with bringing attention back to the question. The participants are asked not to frustrate themselves by trying to keep outside thoughts out and not to try to figure out why they occur, but simply to bring their awareness back to the question each time they notice it has drifted away.

The question is in the foreground of consciousness throughout all activities. When setting out for a walking contemplation, the participants are reminded that they are to walk alone with one thing in mind, their question. Who is walking? Who is breathing? Who is hearing the sounds, smelling the smells, and who is asking the question?

They are reminded during the working meditation that its purpose is to discover who is working. Who is raking the leaves? Who is washing the dishes, sweeping the hall, chopping vegetables? Before eating, they are asked to seek out who it is that is chewing, tasting, and smelling. At the end of the first day, when it is time for bed, they are asked to make their question the last thing that they are conscious of before they fall asleep. There are usually some very tired smiles about the sleeping meditation. But there are dreams to be dreamt and once in a while someone wakes up with the very thing he is looking for.

By the end of the first day everyone has a good idea what an Enlightenment Intensive is about. If someone truly wanted to leave for any reason, this is the time for dropping out. But, by the end of the day, the participants know that the process is working within them and usually all will continue. The master will ask anyone who is not sure at the beginning of the Intensive to remain at least for this first day.

Everyone is tired. It has been a long day. They will sleep easily, yet within the sleep state a heightened state of consciousness is beginning to emerge. Participants say that during the night they are asleep as usual but somehow more awake. They are totally aware of what goes on around them as they sleep. They are aware of anyone walking through the room or turning over in their sleep; but the awareness does not wake them nor disturb their sleep. When they dream, their dreams are clearer, brighter in color, and more easily remembered the morning after.

The second day begins. The participants are asked to tell their partners anything that may have occurred to them during the night or upon awakening. The room seems much clearer. The first day leaves an ambient feeling in the room which sometimes feels like a pea-soup fog. The fog is beginning to clear as thoughts become clarified and feelings begin to emerge.

During the day some of the participants will ask for an interview with the master. They may feel that they are no longer making any progress, or are unsure that they are doing the communication exercise properly. When going into an interview the participant is asked to go into the interview room, sit down facing the master and to act as if the master is just another partner.

'Tell me who you are,' says the master. He does not expect a final answer at this point but wants to see if the participant is following his instructions carefully. John, our hypothetical participant, answers, 'Well, I don't think anything is happening to me. When I ask myself the question nothing happens.'

'What does nothing feel like to you?' replies the master.

'I just close my eyes and there's nothing to see. It gives me a headache to keep thinking of my question, as if I'm pushing myself too hard trying to look for it.'

'What else do you feel in your body?'

'Well, my back aches and I feel anxious sitting in front of you.

It reminds me of when I was in school and I had to report to the teacher or something. I feel absolutely frustrated and lost.'

'Many people feel the same way at this point in the Intensive. I understand how you feel about me being in this position of authority. Do you understand that for the purpose of what we are doing here I am the authority figure and must be, in order to help you find what you are looking for?'

'Yes, I know that. I can feel now after talking to you that it's happening because I've always let outside authorities tell me who I was. I feel angry at them now.'

'It is important to express that to your partner until it changes. Thank you for telling me. Let me review with you again how to do the communication exercise. When your partner gives you the instructions to tell him who you are be sure to take a few seconds to set about experiencing yourself directly before you answer. This is different than attempting to "look" for yourself. Stop looking and intend to know directly. Do you understand the difference?'

'I think so. Is that why I'm getting this headache?" asks John.

'Perhaps. It is not important to determine the exact reason for your headache, or anything that you may be experiencing as a result of your contemplation. It is important, however, to allow yourself to experience it fully and express it in detail to your partner. Tell your partner precisely how your headache feels to you. Do the same with your backache and your frustration, anger, or whatever is happening to you. Where exactly is your headache? How big is it? Does it throb or is it a continuous ache? Allow yourself to go right into the pain of it. Imagine yourself placing the question right over the pain so that you can put your full awareness on both the question and the pain. In this way you can feel it fully, express it precisely to your partner, and allow it to change. Understand that your headache and whatever you feel at this time is a direct result of asking yourself this question.'

'Yes, I see.'

'Since you are not having any thoughts you say that nothing is happening but there is a lot happening in your body, isn't there?'

'Yes, I guess I don't put much consequence on my feelings. As you told us before, I identify more with my thoughts.'

'Make the question one with you. Who is experiencing all this? Who is setting about to experience himself? Who is thinking, "nothing is happening"? Do not change your question but consider these things. Even in the void there is someone experiencing voidness.'

John nods in understanding. He seems more determined and awake now.

'O.K. Now go back and do it.'

'Thank you.'

As the second day continues, the atmosphere of the meditation room undergoes changes. People are encountering the fourth stage, the void and absolute silence occurs for minutes at a time as participants dig even deeper into themselves. Then there are tears and outbursts of emotion as they move into the next stage.

The Intensive is not one but several processes. Throughout there is a process of clarification. During the communication exercises, the participants are clearing their minds of unrelated thoughts and clarifying each concept and thought as it comes up and is communicated to their partner. Vague, half-understood ideas become precise statements.

A process of dis-identification takes place. The participant gets in touch with what he has identified himself as being in the past. He may be identified with some role he has played in life such as 'good guy', or 'a helper', or with some vocation he has had. He may be identified with his mind or his body or his feelings. As he encounters each of his identifications, and communicates them to his partner, the truth or lack of truth in his identifications will become apparent. If the role or identity is basically untrue, it will vanish to the degree that it is communicated to and understood by another.

Toward the end of the process of enlightenment the participant will be presenting himself more and more as he really is in truth. The process of presentation of self is the essence of the self-enlightenment process. At first the participant is trying to answer a question. Then the participant becomes a questioning, his or her whole being is at one with the question. In the final stages he or she becomes the answer. The enlightenment takes place when the participant is presenting himself or herself fully as truth to others. Along with the enlightenment come a few words which for the participant at that time are totally appropriate to describing who he is. But the words are secondary to the actual presentation of himself or herself as the answer.

Another aspect of the process is love. Although the participants do not have conversations in the normal socializing way, they are in the act of revealing themselves to others. This is a good definition of love: to reveal yourself to another and accept unconditionally what another reveals to you. By the end of the intensive the meditation room is filled with affinity and love. It is a strange occurrence because many of the participants do not even know each others' names, or what the others are like in the outside world. This process of opening up to others is what makes the Enlightenment Intensive work so rapidly and deeply.

The process is not just one of answering a question. The question is just a tool. The question is the map, the truth is the target. By analogy, the question is like a magnet on the end of a fishing line. By 'holding the question' you drop your line with its magnetic bait into the unconscious. The unconsious is like a barrel full of old artefacts and furniture, and scrap metal. The question pulls to it only those things which are connected to the idea 'Who am I?' The line is reeled in. The things from the unconscious which cling to the bait are collected one at a time and shown to another (your partner). When the magnetic bait is cleaned of its catch, it is once again lowered into the unconscious. There it collects more things, things which where hidden before. It is like emptying out a barrel. At the bottom of the barrel is a mirror. When revealed and polished, it reflects a true image of the seeker to himself.

By the end of the second day, or the beginning of the third, some participants begin to have the experiences that they are seeking. The enlightenment experience is different for everyone. Some have outrageous explosions of feeling and some slide into it like sliding into a relaxing warm bath. One thing is common to everyone. There is no doubt about who one is, and there is a centered tranquility about oneself. They feel themselves from the top of their heads to the soles of their feet and there is no separation of body and mind, or thoughts and feelings. They usually realize along with it that they are who they are, and always have been, no matter what they are thinking, feeling, or doing. The contact between themselves and others and their environment is deep and clear. Their faces are alive with inner radiance. Their very presence can be felt as one feels the surrounding temperature of the air.

The Degrees of Enlightenment

There is one kind of enlightenment: direct experience of the truth. There are, however, many degrees of enlightenment. A person who has experienced the answer to the question 'Who am I?' at one point in his life may work again on the same question at a later time and gain a deeper degree of enlightenment concerning his true nature.

In my own process, and in my experience as an enlightenment master, (a role I am not attached to in normal life) I have seen how enlightenment experiences go deeper and deeper. In describing these degrees or depths of enlightenment I want to remind the reader that the words that a participant gives as the answer to his or her enlightenment are only of secondary importance to the experience itself. The words are important in that they help to communicate the experience to others. But the words are not the experience itself, and this varies from person to person. Having had many people for Intensives over several years, I have seen a pattern emerge out of their answers. At each degree of enlightenment there is a consistency in the verbal answers given. They are either very similar or exactly the same. The answers give an idea as to the degree or depth of the individual's experience.

First let us consider the process of self-enlightenment, using the questions, 'Who am I?', 'What am I?', or 'What is my true nature?' Invariably the answers are of the following kind: 'I am', 'I am me', 'I am myself', or simply, 'Me'. In the first degree of self-enlightenment the answers are simply self-evident, the kind of answer you would get if you asked a young child who he is; he would look at you as if you were very stupid and say, 'I'm me of course'.

The answers given in the first degree of life-enlightenment are similar to those for self-enlightenment in that they make a self-evident statement of simplicity. The questions are: 'What is Life?', What is the purpose of Life?', or 'How is Life fulfilled?' The answers to these questions are usually: 'This!', 'Life is!', 'Living!', or 'The purpose of Life is living', or 'Life is fulfilled by living.'

It is not that these answers were unknown to the participants before they came to an Enlightenment. Many gave these answers to their partners in the first hour of the Intensive. The difference is that, after their enlightenment, they are in direct conscious awareness of the incredible fact of their own existence or the existence of life. Their whole being is experiencing it 'now'. Before the enlightenment they only had the *idea* that they existed or that life existed. And so, although their statements are simple, they are profound.

What this process points out to me time and time again is the sad condition of most of humanity. Most people go through their whole lives surrounded by the deadening field of their own mentality. They are not really alive, but caught in a subdued world of ideas and roles which keeps them out of direct contact with the amazing and wonderful fact of life itself.

The first degree of enlightenment for the question 'What is another?' is similar in that, for the first time, the experience of the fact of another's existence is experienced. The answers given by participants run along lines like, 'Another is!' If you are concerned why the world is in such a sorry state of affairs, or why so many people can ignore the existence of so many others, or why so many of us are lonely so much of the time, then consider this question and its answer.

The great majority of us do not really contact each other directly but, instead, choose to keep people as objects in our minds. It is only in specific situations under special circumstances that we allow ourselves direct and intimate contact with another. To most of us people are things, objects to be dealt with through the façades of our personalities and belief systems. Business, politics, or power are always more immediate and important to a person who does not have the consciousness that another actually exists. Another person is the source of life's most fulfilling experiences – love and friendship.

The direct, fully conscious, experience of another's existence is something that can change your life. A new respect and caring for others arises which is far beyond the mentally produced role of a 'person who cares for others' with which we are all familiar.

The questions are rotated in such a manner that the participant who continues coming to Intensives will work on them in this order: first he must answer, 'Who am I?' or another of the self-enlightenment questions. Then he can go on to 'What is Life?', followed by 'What is another?' Then he returns to the first question to seek a deeper degree of self-enlightenment. It is not uncommon for a participant to answer several questions during a three or five day Intensive. (Intensives sometimes run from five to twenty-one days.)

The second degree of self-enlightenment occurs when a participant goes beyond the simple fact of his existence to seek the nature, the *what*, of the 'I am'. The process is similar to that which brought him to the first degree, but he has more confidence in the process and knows that he has the ability to find out. It usually takes him a shorter period of time to gain it.

The answers that come out of the second degree of self-enlightenment are astounding: 'I am the source of me', 'I am the God of my universe', or simply, 'I am God'. In other context, these answers could help one land in some institution under observation. But these people are not insane. They are in fact more sane than they have ever been. The experience of being the creator of the 'outer me' is like the experience of being what Western minds think of as God. The second degree of self-enlightenment is characterized by a realization that you are totally responsible for who you are. This is at once a great responsibility to assume and a freeing experience. For once you take responsibilty for how you are, then, and only then, can you change it.

The second degree of life-enlightenment also has the additional quality of responsibility. The question, although used in its original form, becomes 'What is life beyond just the surviving and living of it?' The answers state directly, or imply, that there is an underlying purpose for life. Its first purpose is of course to live it as fully as you can. Its second purpose is to become conscious of yourself and others. Answers arise, such as 'Life is a relationship that all beings have with one another', 'The purpose of life is love', 'The purpose of life is growth', or 'Life is the way we can meet each other'.

The question has two sides which merge into each other. 'What is the purpose of life in general and what is the purpose in my life in particular?' The deeper the enlightenment into the nature of life, the more you find that life is a means of growth and that growth is intimately connected with your relationship with others. The answers indicate that life is fulfilled by deepening contact with your environment, especially other people. A further question asks you to examine the things you are doing in your own life: 'Are you fulfilling life as well as you can?' Most of the people who come to an Enlightenment Intensive discover that they are already fulfilling life by seeking greater contact with themselves, life and others. After this degree of enlightenment, they may decide to organize their lives in such a way that they can participate more directly in life, and perhaps aid others in doing so.

Life-enlightenment brings you to a state of consciousness where you transcend the barriers of your private world and feel yourself to be intimately connected to all things. It is a feeling of universal brotherhood, and love for the earth upon which we all live and grow. The deeper your life-enlightenment goes, the more it points out to you in specific, here-and-now terms, the purpose of your personal and trans-personal life. It is not just a belief but an inner knowing that fills your being.

The second degree of enlightenment concerning another is exemplified by a deep realization that not only does another exist but another is a unique individual whose nature is identical with your own. This is a difficult thing to put into words. The 'Who' of the other is absolutely unique. He or she is completely another person. Yet, at the same time, both of you share the same nature. As consciousness grows, an appreciation of both the differences between people and the sameness of their natures grows along with it. It is a dichotomy which cannot be handled easily by the conceptual mind, but one that can be experienced directly.

The deepest stage or degree of self-enlightenment is exemplified by the answers, 'I am ability', 'I am the "I can".' But the words are only an indication of what lies behind them. In this state, you experience your true nature apart from all things conceptual. You experience yourself as being essentially a non-physical being who is not composed of anything such as matter or energy, thought or feeling. Not being a thing, you have no shape or form which is you. You experience yourself as having always existed and therefore being without prior source. You see that your mind, body and physical universe are all your creations. These are things which you use to communicate with, but they are, essentially, not you. The closest English equivalent to what you are is the word 'ability'. But you do not have ability. Ability is what you are. You experience yourself as limitless and boundless, yet centered in the here-and-now.

The personal experience is one of realizing that the real you is not your brain or your conceptual ability. The functions of thinking and feeling are initiated by you from a deeper source within. Although you are centered mostly in your body, in order to participate in life, you extend, in physical terms, to the far reaches of the universe.

Now we are getting into concepts that cannot be understood except through experience. The third stage or degree of self-enlightenment requires a complete transcendence of rational thought. The mind alone cannot come up with the concepts that are described above. They describe a reality that seems, at first glance, to be unreal with respect to our normal perception of the world. If we accept them as truth, then our whole picture of reality will have to change.

To describe what reality looks like from within the deeper stages of enlightenment is what I have attempted to outline in Psychometaphysics. The enlightenment experience itself, however, takes place in a timeless instant, outside the bounds of conceptual thought. To describe it in words would take another book if, indeed, it could be written down.

Postscript

The stated purpose of the Enlightenment Intensive is to gain a direct experience of the nature of you, life, and others. In the long run, however, the purpose becomes much more than that. In continuing to do Intensives over a period of years, I have found that it is also a method of developing the ability to know things from oneself.

The process of knowing things from oneself is a form of meditation. It is dependent on the asking of a question, or the intent to experience a particular thing. A scientist or mathematician uses the same process to solve a problem. He will steep himself in the question at hand and then, at some later time, the answer will pop into consciousness, perhaps in sleep or some other unexpected time. What scientists would not be inclined to admit is that this process falls under the heading of mysticism. The current connotation of the word mysticism implies that it is a way of hiding things behind a façade of imprecise religious jargon. But that is not what mysticism really is. The mystic is someone who has trained his mind and body to give him a clear experience and understanding of sensual reality.

Imagine if science were able, at some time in the distant future, to produce a machine which could accurately detect and organize all phenomena in the universe. The machine would represent the culmination of scientific instrumentation technology. It would measure and compute all things, from the smallest to the infinitely large, and bring into focus all frequencies of whatever forces exist, no matter how weak or strong they are. The machine would give science an accurate and precise picture of the universe. Mystics know that this machine already exists. Every human being on earth is walking around in one.

How is it that an individual can perceive beyond the accepted boundaries of his perceptual senses? The answer is simple, if you have direct knowledge of your own essential nature. The nature of the 'I' is such that it is not simply an observer of the universe. It is also the creator, or more accurately, the co-creator of the universe. So, on a very deep level, each of us knows everything, since we have put it there. Have the thought of a triangle in your mind. How do you know it is there?

The problem is not one of gaining knowledge but of making the knowledge you already have conscious to your waking self. This is done simply (not necessarily easily or quickly) by ridding your body-mind of all fixities. The things that keep you from knowing are manifold. You must clear your mind of all fixed attitudes or viewpoints. You must learn not to place value on any part of yourself or life to the detriment of any other part. You must clear your body of toxicity and tensions, especially the chronic, which distort its perceptions. You must clear up your relationships with others so that you are presenting yourself as you truly are. Then you can direct your consciousness to answer any question you like, starting with self, life and others. There's no way of getting around it. The process of becoming a mystic is the same process as personal growth. So, why call it mystical?

References

1. Manley P. Hall, *Cabalistic Keys to the Lord's Prayer*, Philosophical Research Society, Los Angeles.

2. Dion Fortune, *The Mystical Qabalah*, Ernest Benn, London, 1970.

3. Carlos Suarès, *The Spectograms of the Hebrew Alphabet*, in collaboration with F. A. Wolf for English translation, unpublished.

4. Paul Foster Case, *The Tarot, A Key to the Wisdom of the Ages*, Macoy, Richmond, Virginia, 1947.

5. Paul Foster Case, *The Book of Tokens*, Builders of the Adytum, Los Angeles, 1968.

6. The relationship between the four elements and the four Tarot suits are from a lecture given by Samuel Bousky at Bridge Mountain Foundation, Ben Lomond, California, 1969.

7. Christian D. Ginsburg, *The Kabbalah, Its Doctrines, Development and Literature*, Routledge & Kegan Paul, London, 1971.

8. Manley P. Hall, *The Secret Teachings of All Ages*, Philosophical Research Society, Los Angeles, 1968.

9. As note 3 above.

10. Carlos Suarès, *The Cipher of Genesis*, Stuart & Watkins, London, 1970, and Bantam, U.S.A.

11. *The Unity Dictionary* or *The Metaphysical Bible Dictionary*, The Unity School of Christianity, Lee's Summit, Missouri, 1951.

12. James Strong, *Srong's Exhaustive Concordance of the Bible*, Hodder & Stoughton, London.

13. Maxwell Maltz, *Psychocybernetics*, Wilshire Books Co. North Hollywood, California.

14. Pierre Teilhard De Chardin, *The Phenomenon of Man*, Collins, London, 1959.

15. Frederick S. Pearls, *Gestalt Therapy Verbatum*, Real People Press, Utah, U.S.A.

16. Roberto Assagioli, *Psychosynthesis, A Manual of Principles and Techniques*, Turnstone Books, London, 1975.

17. *The Superconscious and The Self*, James Vargiu, Psychosynthesis Institute, Redwood City, California, 1973.

18. C. C. Zain, *The Sacred Tarot*, The Church of Light, Los Angeles, 1966.

19. Philip Kapleau, *The Pillars of Zen*, Beacon, U.S.A., 1967.

Biographical Note

Jeff Love (his real name) has been leading groups using the methods of Humanistic Psychology since 1969. He has been involved in the establishing and running of several communities and centers based on the process of personal growth. Among these are Bridge Mountain Foundation in California, Center in Amsterdam, and Finca La Follenca in Spain, Europe's first fully residential growth center.

Although he has wide experience in many of the approaches of Humanistic Psychology – such as Gestalt, Encounter, Bioenergetics – his speciality is the Enlightenment Intensive process as developed by Charles Berner. He introduced the Enlightenment Intensive format to Europe in 1972.

Before he became interested in psychology as a career, Jeff was an architectural-interior designer with a background in architectural engineering. While making the transition from engineer to psychologist, he became interested in the Qabalah and its logical geometrical approach to philosophical theology. He believes that metaphysics was the psychology of pre-nineteenth century civilizations and that it still holds important keys to understanding the nature of twentieth century man.